# Combining Scales for REALISTIC DIORAMAS

by Enrique Carrasco

Kalmbach Media
21027 Crossroads Circle
Waukesha, Wisconsin 53186
www.KalmbachHobbyStore.com



All photos were taken by the author, unless otherwise noted.

Please follow appropriate health and safety measures when working with materials and equipment. Some general guidelines are presented in this book, but always read and follow the manufacturers' instructions.

Published in 2022
26 25 24 23 22   1 2 3 4 5

Manufactured in China

ISBN: 978-1-62700-902-7
EISBN: 978-1-62700-903-4

Cover Photos: Enrique Carrasco Molina
Editor: Mark Savage
Book Design: Lisa Schroeder

Library of Congress Control Number: 2021952726

# Contents

# Combining scales as an innovation in the design and creation of dioramas

**The scale model and diorama market is constantly evolving.** Modelers are looking for, and asking for, more sophisticated accessories, while making ever more realistic dioramas. But many modelers face the problem of not having enough space to display, or store, their finished dioramas in their homes. This has led many to eliminate the vehicles (tanks, cars, boats, planes) or to design smaller vignettes, instead of large dioramas, all to save space.

The market has reacted to this trend toward vignettes by selling sections of vehicles, buildings, etc., to be posed in these smaller scenes, which certainly can still be artistic. Likewise, the concept of combining scales can help modelers create impressive dioramas in a smaller space. Mixing scales can create interesting scenarios, including vehicles, while employing depth of field. This technique also allows modelers to take attractive photographs with a nod toward realism.

Recently some classic model brands, such as Lindberg, Hasegawa, and Revell, have sold kits mixing vehicles of different scales that play to modelers wanting to create mixed-scale dioramas. Likewise, some expert modelers have published books discussing dioramas, including box dioramas, and isolated examples of combined-scale scenes. A few have written about forced-perspective dioramas too, although those primarily focus on photographing dioramas. Rarely has there been a large, specialized book explaining the concepts of mixed-scale dioramas while also including detailed step-by-step examples.

This is that book.

Here I include my concepts for the scenes, but also all the information needed to create a similar diorama. That includes detailed information about the tools used in all the projects, such as brushes, mini drills, sandpaper, scissors, airbrushes, cutting devices of all types, etc. I also include the techniques used, such as patinas or washes, dry-brushing, touches with pastel pencils, the tonal effect that rises with different color ranges along with all the special materials used, such as resins, paints, varnishes, putties. ground cover elements, artificial grass, and snow. It's a long list.

My projects also introduce new techniques for creating realistic ground surfaces, water, etc. A few new, possibly unusual, techniques include using breath mints to imitate ice, tinfoil for blankets, layered tissues and other items for clothing, silicone and resins for water, crayons to brighten a portion of the sea, shoe polish to age wood, and cotton swabs to imitate an old building's columns. Creativity is the key to realistic and unique dioramas.

This book strives to provide an innovative vision of diorama design and construction. To that end helpful tips are provided for modelers who want to improve the realism of the photos they take of their work, by finding interesting camera angles to best play off the perspective created by combining various model scales. Here you'll find seven step-by-step projects, an introductory chapter, and more than 300 color photos along with a discussion of a variety of modeling methods, painting techniques and scene creation, plus the creation of figures in realistic poses.

All revolve around multiscale dioramas, effective use of backgrounds, and proper lighting effects to be captured in photos that make your diorama come to life.

Finally, this book helps the reader learn about a variety of important civil and military moments in history across different civilizations, and how to re-create those times in a convincing diorama.

In this sense, it includes examples of Hanseatic trade in the Middle Ages, a naval scene during the Roman Empire, and an episode of the 80 Years' War in Belgium's Flanders. Likewise there are two important scenes from United States history, the first an early episode, when Pedro Menéndez de Avilés sails to Florida and the famous scene of Gen. George Washington crossing the Delaware River, a diorama inspired by the famous painting by Emanuel Gottlieb Leutze (1851). It is the first time that this scene has been made with this complexity and this scale. My step-by-step process will help you make your own version.

Modelers interested in more current historical events will find two chapters focusing on World War II's Battle of the Bulge in the Ardennes. One reflects the experiences of German troops and their air support, while the other presents a stressed patrol of US soldiers, both in cold, wintry scenes.

I hope you enjoy it.

Enrique Carrasco

Thank you to all my family and friends, for
everyone's patience and understanding of this hobby.
To my colleague José María López Lago, who suggested the idea
of a Washington Crossing the Delaware diorama.
To my son Joaquín for helping me in photographing the projects, and to my other
son Enrique and to María, for their patience and support.

Credits

Models, dioramas and photos: Enrique Carrasco Molina.
Naval Advisor: Francisco Javier Carrasco Molina.
Aviation Advisor: Secundino Elías Darias García
Proofreading and revision: Isabella Vidal Rodríguez.
Photos: All photos taken by the author, except as noted.

## ACKNOWLEDGEMENTS

This book would not have become a reality without the support of the Kalmbach Media and *FineScale Modeler* teams. Thanks for the support of Eric White and Aaron Skinner from the beginning, Mark Savage for his editing skills, and Lisa Schroeder for her dynamic layout design.

Thanks to all my modeling friends, to Zona Modelista (Alex Curiá, Javier Labory and Secundino Elías Darias), for their advice, and to Club de Maquetistas de Tenerife, for inspiring and encouraging me, forever.

# Combining scales to create the illusion of depth

**A primary goal** when combining model scales in dioramas is to be able to take realistic photos with great depth of field. To accomplish this, one must focus on where to place the diorama's major elements.

The table at right shows the different scales used in this book's projects, some are well known and readily available commercially. Those include 1/16, 1/32, 1/35, 1/72, 1/56, and 1/87. Others are less common, such as 1/20, 1/160 or 1/600.

I have not established a specific technical table of distances (inches) for placing each element in an individual diorama. Instead, I experiment with photo tests as I establish my scenes. I first place the figures, vehicles, buildings, airplanes, etc. on a base and adjust the distances separating them to find the best organization and photo angles. Gluing in place comes much later.

Doing these photo tests allow the diorama builder to make sure key elements are not too far apart from each other so that, when taking environmental photographs, you can play with lighting, vanishing points, and depth of field. That means trying to keep the foreground, middle zone, and background as much in focus as possible. When the diorama is finished and you photograph the diorama you can still help the images with various types of software, such as Photoshop, to retouch the pictures. Tools such as "focus" or "focus more," can work alongside the scaled scenery to help generate the illusion of realistic depth.

Here we see in the side view image atop page 7 the distance between the figures, 7.87 inches between the soldier in the foreground (1/16 scale) and the first of the soldiers by the house (1/35 scale). The space between the two soldiers next to the barn is 4.3 inches. The front view below that illustrates the different angles and locations where one could position the camera to take realistic photos that combine both scales and do not lose the illusion of reality. The arrows indicate the different camera positions possible without losing depth of field.

## Scale Combination Table

** Two scales combined in diorama., *** Three scales combined in diorama

|  |  |  |  |
|---|---|---|---|
| | 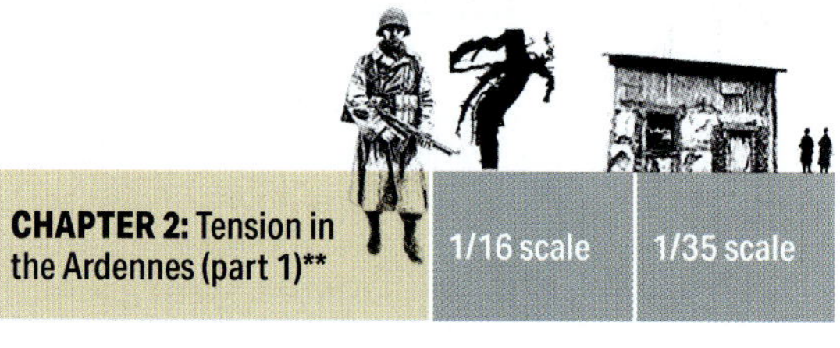 | | |
| **CHAPTER 2:** Tension in the Ardennes (part 1)** | 1/16 scale | 1/35 scale | |
| |  | | |
| **CHAPTER 3:** Tension in the Ardennes (part 2)** | 1/35 scale | 1/72 scale | |
| |  | | |
| **CHAPTER 4:** George Washington crossing the Delaware River*** | 1/32 scale | 1/56 scale | 1/72 scale |
| |  | | |
| **CHAPTER 5:** Siege of Rheinberg (1856-1590)*** | 1/32 scale | 1/35 scale | 1/72 scale |
| |  | | |
| **CHAPTER 6:** Pedro Menendez de Aviles sails to Florida ** | 1/35 scale | 1/600 scale | |
| |  | | |
| **CHAPTER 7:** Trade with the Hanseatic League** | 1/72 scale | 1/87 scale | |
| |  | | |
| **CHAPTER 8:** Pax Romana** | 1/20 scale | 1/160 scale | |

In this diorama featuring a German AB43 and a Focke-Wulf Fw 190D-9, I worked with two scales, 1/35 and 1/72, which is discussed in detail in Chapter 3. The two are placed very closely together in the final photo to keep both in focus, while the aircraft was hung in the sky with a thick wire, taking advantage of the ambient light to create an interesting and realistic result.

## CHAPTER ONE

# An introduction to depth of field in multiscale dioramas

**This book grew from my own modeling aspirations.** I wanted to create a series of projects that had long been on my mind and having to do with the visual depth used to create dioramas that draw the viewers into the scene, what some call multiscale or forced-perspective dioramas created by combining models of various scales. I was especially interested in creating accurate depth when taking realistic-looking photos of my dioramas.

I first worked on marine scenes using two different scales, combining an interesting 1/20 scale human figure with an attractive scale ship. I posed the figure on a sort of terrace, looking down at a 1/200 scale docked galleon, then took a photo (above). The result was simple, but relatively effective combining the two scales and that motivated me to keep experimenting on future dioramas (some included in this book).

But I soon realized that if I wanted to give personality to a scene using figures dressed in historically accurate clothing, and bigger than 1/72 scale, the dioramas would end up being way too big to store and display at home. I had to find a solution. The answer was learning how different scale objects could combine properly in the same scene on a manageable-sized base (see image at right).

Almost immediately I came to a conclusion that would guide my construction of future dioramas. Scales such as 1/35 or 1/32 match well with sailing ship kits between 1/200 and 1/600 scale posed on a 50-inch x 50-inch base. I then experimented with combining different spatial scales until I found an acceptable angle for taking realistic pictures.

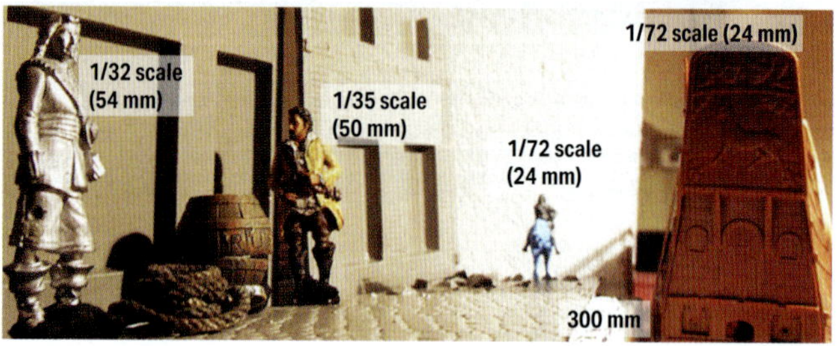


I also found that to create a realistic effect I had to work with various light sources to find one that allows the eye to accept the composition as if it were in true perspective.

One reason many modelers don´t combine different scales is because their goal is to create a simple tabletop diorama easily shown at a contest and where viewers can look at the diorama from various perspectives. While building a diorama using multiple scales forces the viewer to look at the diorama from one specific angle, unless the diorama is placed in a box or container that allows just one viewing angle, this becomes difficult for dioramas displayed at contests.

A model of the 18th century French ship *Le Gladiateur* (1/200 scale) is used here to simulate a docked ship while a woman carrying a pitcher (1/32 scale) walks toward us. Just looking at the picture it's difficult to know the actual distance between the ship and the figure, but the sunset lighting helps separate the ship from its background, increasing the realism. You do not need much distance between the figure and ship, at most 2 inches.

**A 15-inch square base and a boat of barely 6 inches were used (Pyro made this 1/600 scale Spanish galleon). Both figures were made from scratch in 1/35 scale. Although the distance between the boat and the ship is only about 10 inches, an illusion of depth is created by combining the two scales and photographing it with a wide-angle lens. Here also you see the detail of the ship's captain. This is just a preliminary rendering of the diorama that you can find in Chapter 6.**

However, never say never.

There is a field that naturally incorporates traditional deep perspective (with the combination of various scales)—nativity scenes. For years people have been creating these. It is common to see dioramas about the birth of Jesus Christ in which the viewer can see large figures of Jesus, Mary and Joseph, produced at a scale of 1/10 to 1/6, and the background, houses, palm trees, camels, or castles at much smaller scales, such as 1/20, 1/25, or 1/32.

Likewise, to create an even more detailed diorama, sometimes it's best to use three scales within a scene. One of my early experiments, made prior to the example of the Flanders war diorama that is shown in Chapter 5, combined three scales: 1/32 for a carriage, knight, and dog, 1/35 for a soldier walking with a donkey, and 1/72 for a rider at the scene's rear.

With the naked eye it is difficult to determine the distances in the first and second groups, for example, or the distance between the first figure and the last one (see the

**We can appreciate the interesting differences of scale that are perfectly integrated into this nativity scene's landscape. The size and depth of the diorama also help the viewer to properly perceive the blending of the different scales. A painted background, imitating distant dunes, increases the sense of visual depth. The smaller palm trees in the background also help create the same optical effect.**
Craftsman: Florencio Pérez, Caja Canarias, 2014.

image on page 14). But it is easy to see how on a relatively small base (no more than 16 inches) a scene can be created with realistic depth when using the correct combination of different-scale figures.

I recommend common commercial kit scales, especially naval, (1/150, 1/200, 1/350, 1/400, 1/600, 1/700, and 1/1200) that can be combined on square bases of from 6 to 20 inches. (See the charts on page 14)

Traditional modelers have basically distinguished between two types of scale staging: open dioramas (on a table, with limited vertical backgrounds, and that can be viewed from

**Although many examples in this book cover marine environments, using various scales in a diorama is practical for modelers who work with classic 1/35 scale military vehicles. Here we see a diorama made by the Canarian modeler Javier Labory, who provided this image to show the depth-of-field effect that can be achieved by combining 1/35 and 1/72 scale models in a World War II desert scene.**

**In this experiment I used three different scales to imply depth, although in the final project I left out the dog and wagon. See more on this project in Chapter 5.**

many angles) and box or closed dioramas, which represent a complete scene with a background and can only be seen from the front, or one perspective. These forced-perspective, or box, dioramas were the favorite of famous modeler and author, the late Sheperd (Shep) Paine. He considered them the epitome of a great diorama.

Some authors believe that dioramas using the combination of scales proposed in this book could only be effective for viewers if in a "dark box," that is, by enclosing the diorama in a box and creating an artificial atmosphere inside that simulates reality. That works, of course, but in the case of large-format dioramas, and naval or landscape dioramas, with a tendency to open display, I believe that this is not necessary for two reasons:

a) In a show or contest the combined-scale diorama is presented with an explanatory label that instructs viewers to look at the diorama from a specific angle so that they understand and appreciate the depth of field created by integrating the different scales.

b) The concept of a combined-scale diorama is closely linked to its photographic use to achieve realistic compositions with adequate backgrounds and lighting.

Certainly there are quite a few famous modelers around the world who have developed innovative projects in the past couple decades that create depth of field in their dioramas by using photographic backgrounds, real landscape backgrounds, lighting effects, different scale kits, and box dioramas. Many have published books telling of their experiences, often inspired by movies and the special effects seen in them. The multiscale examples that these modelers have developed in recent years, stand out in different fields and genres of classical modeling, but they often break old schemes with the creative exploration of materials and the technological innovation of photography to create stunning final results.

## SCALE EQUIVALENCES

**These two tables of scale equivalences help show which dimension we can work with to create proper scale in a diorama. Although the equivalences are correct, slightly different ratios apply using traditional model scales. (You can see slight differences between both tables). We can indicate combinations that could work well as an example in dioramas that are specifically designed using various scale combinations. At first glance, the eye interprets the depth to the extent that we are placing the different objects at different points. An example: In the diorama at left, if we placed the soldier with the donkey (1/35 scale) farther back, the depth effect would be lost because it would lose dimension and focus, especially if the intention is to photograph the scene.**

| Height (mm) | Scale |
|---|---|
| 4.6 | 1/350 |
| 5.6 | 1/285 |
| 6 | 1/268 |
| 8 | 1/200 |
| 10 | 1/150 |
| 11.2 | 1/144 |
| 15 | 1/107 |
| 16.1 | 1/100 |
| 18.5 | 1/87 |
| 20 | 1/80.5 |
| 22 | 1/73 |
| 25 | 1/64 |
| 28 | 1/58 |
| 30 | 1/54 |
| 33.5 | 1/48 |
| 40 | 1/40 |
| 54 | 1/30 |
| 70 | 1/23 |
| 75 | 1/21.5 |
| 80 | 1/20 |
| 90 | 1/18 |
| 100.6 | 1/16 |

| Height (mm) | Scale |
|---|---|
| 25 | 1:72 |
| 30 | 1:60 |
| 49 | 1:35 |
| 54 | 1:32 |
| 60 | 1:30 |
| 75 | 1:24 |
| 90 | 1:18 |
| 120 | 1:15/1:16 |

# Brilliant examples of dioramas that use depth of field to create realism

There are some brilliant examples of depth of field in dioramas. Ivan Kangur's projects are interesting, involving airplanes and spaceships presented in dioramas with illuminated backgrounds contrasted with dynamic speed elements. Then there are the attractive vintage cars and gas station scenes created by Ignacio Pérez and Sebastián Pérez (modeljunkyard.com) that are photographed with a real landscape in the background, taking advantage of the distant shapes of trees or mountains. Dioramas by New Jersey's Matthew Albanese involve strange landscapes and worlds (*Strange Worlds*) decorated with spectacular cloud compositions made with cotton and amazing light effects.

When it comes to creating models and photos essential to our understanding of how the human eye can be deceived by illusion, perspective, and contrasting scales, the late Michael Paul Smith of Pennsylvania was remarkable. Along the same lines, so are David Griffith's naval dioramas that create stunningly realistic scenes both in port and offshore while using warships and peacetime vessels.

Amazing too is Norwegian Bjorn Jacobsen, who creates military scenes and realistic battles full of explosions depicted by using cotton and special lighting effects, in addition to prepared backgrounds. Another is Joseph M. Neumeyer, who worked on a concept of depth and movement that he called "dynamic dioramas." He even collaborated in producing miniatures in several science fiction movies.

These modelers have published their ideas in various books:

-Bjorn Jacobsen has published several books, including *A Tutorial for Making Military Dioramas and Models*, vols. 1-4, self, ISBN 979-8688477962 (2020 edition)

-Michael Paul Smith and Gail K. Ellison authored *Elgin Park, Visual Memories of Midcentury America at 1/24th scale*, Animal Media Group, ISBN 978-1947895140

-David Griffith created *Ship Dioramas: Bringing Your Models to Life*, Seaforth, ISBN 978-1848321687

-Matthew Albanese offers the extraordinary *Strange Worlds*, Lazy Dog Press, ISBN 978-8898030033

Perhaps some of the modelers who contrast small objects, such as houses and cars, with real street views or landscapes and then photograph the whole set from realistic angles, were inspired by trompe l'oeil, an ancient pictorial technique dating back to the 15th century. Its intent was to fool the eye by playing with the architectural environment (real or simulated), perspective, shading, and other optical effects, achieving an intensified reality or reality substitution. Let's look briefly at the early attempts at creating depth of field in the fine arts.

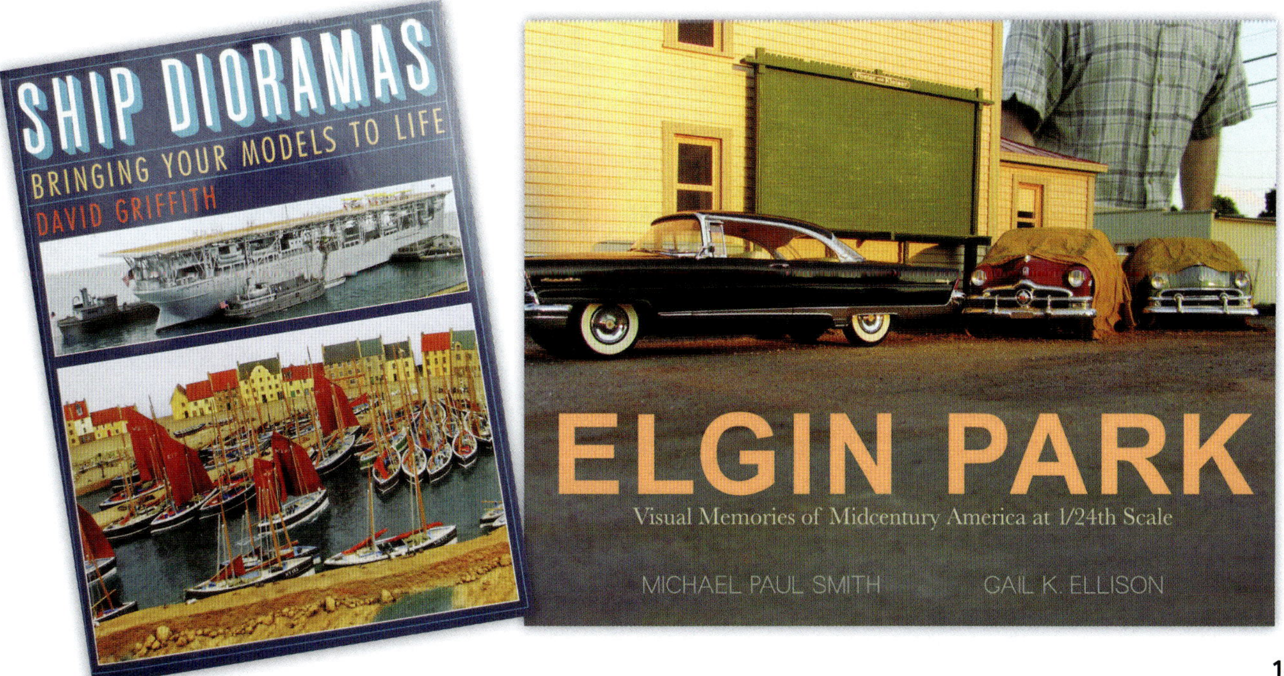

# Depth of field in the fine arts, a brief history

Depth of field and its application to fine arts (and applied arts) has its own history. It would take another book to analyze the history of perspectives and depth of field in fine arts, in paintings, the theater, and sculpture (reliefs are a clear example of the unlimited possibilities of combining figures of different sizes.

The possibilities of distorting perspectives and backgrounds in paintings have been known since ancient times. Also classical theater in Greece and Rome allowed great creativity to deceive the viewer with curtains, painted backgrounds, and elements of the decoration that suggested depth. The same exists today in most theater productions' sets.

At the end of the 18th century and first decades of the 19th century, important experiments were carried out to re-create scenery with artificial depth and panoramic views, with the influence of the theater, fine decoration, and different painting techniques (examples are Cyclorama, Myriorama, Panorama or Panoramic painting). One of these experiments was the *Eidophusikon* (**top of page 18**),

*View of the Government House and Patio de Armas in the Surinam Colony and part of Fort Zelandia* was a unique diorama enclosed in a wooden box made in the 19th century through a concept of depth similar to that of the current dark box dioramas. It is described as "the view over the square of Suriname from the southwest." In the background we see the Suriname River, where you can see boats and Fort Zelandia flying the British Union Jack. The scene's creator has played with perspective, with different elements such as the landscape, the buildings, as well as the figures and the boats.
Image: Rijksmuseum, 1812. Wikimedia Commons

devised by David Garrick, a French painter, and designed by Philippe Jacques de Loutherbourg. It was a large-scale miniature theater that allowed experimentation in an attempt to create the perfect illusion of natural reality: scenes of sunrise, sunset, moonlight, storms, and volcanoes accompanied by sound effects and music. It opened in London's Leicester Square in February 1781.

As exhibited at the National Maritime Museum in Greenwich, England, there is a kind of rudimentary (but realistic) box diorama or dioramic model that was made in 1783 and whose design probably had its influence on the launch of the Eidophusikon. It is a box adorned with a gold frame depicting Admiral Rodney's victory at the Battle of the Saints in 1782. The scene is based on an oil painting by Richard Paton and combines the false perspective and a painting on glass inside the box, to present the climax of the battle, including the interaction of cannon fire, smoke and fire. The museum's label explains "the design seems to show the influence of Loutherbourg's mechanical theater, *The Eidophusikon*, as recorded by the drawing of E.F. Burney," according to the British Museum in London.

But it was not until the advent of photography in the 19th century when the possibilities of creating more realistic scenes and simulated backgrounds were explored more fully. The use of techniques such as slideshows or performances based on video art have now led to sophisticated techniques in digital photography and the improvement of images thanks to photo retouching computer programs such Photoshop.

Louis Daguerre was one of the first to study the best way to capture a portion of landscape through a photo and then create a false depth of field to increase the sense of realism. This French artist and photographer was the first to use the term diorama, now a favorite of modelers. Daguerre coined the term in 1822 for a type of rotating exhibit that later was popularized in the late 19th and early 20th century by Frank Chapman, associate curator at the American Museum of Natural History.

***The Eidophusikon*, A view of Philip James de Loutherbourg's Eidophusikon at the British Museum in London, 1783.** Image: Wikimedia Commons

More recently museums have expanded their exhibit space used for dioramas, decorative settings and performances. It is the most realistic way to explain history, famous battles, or scenes of daily life in different eras. Some exhibits feature isolated models, others box dioramas, and some large, more complex dioramas including figures or mannequins presented in 1/1 scale in front of painted backgrounds. In many cases the museums create artistic backgrounds and special effects to visually trick the viewers in hopes of creating a more realistic experience. Not surprisingly, many museums hire expert modelers to create these scenes from scratch.

**French artist and photographer Louis Daguerre.** Collection of George Eastman House, International Museum of Photography and Film (1844).

**Spectators watch a Daguerre diorama.** Images: Wikimedia Commons

# Classic brand kits made for combined-scale projects

Through the years some classic model brands, such as Revell, Lindberg, and Hasegawa, have created kits that included vehicles of different scales that could be used in creating dioramas. Some even combined aircraft and warships in the same kit. These multiscale kits probably had, as a marketing strategy, the goal of stimulating the imagination of the modeler to help him or her compose dioramas: for example, by re-creating in a small way the attack on Pearl Harbor, or the famous U.S. Civil War battle between he Merrimack and the Monitor at Hampton Roads, Va.

We hope the examples in this book help stimulate modelers' creativity when it comes to diorama building. One also could hope it encourages model manufacturers to create new combo-kits containing airplanes, ships, tanks, buildings, horses or figures of different scales to continue generating new ideas for the creation of multiscale dioramas.

Top to bottom, the Yamato battleship in 1/450 scale and Zero in 1/72 scale; vintage 1956 Revell Merchant Fleet kit (scales not listed, but it contains a Harbor Tug in larger scale than the ships); Lindberg's Monitor and Merrimack in mixed scales; and Revell's Pearl Harbor Attack Set with 1/426 scale Missouri and 1/72 scale Kate attack bomber.

## CHAPTER TWO

PART 1

# Tension in the Ardennes

**SKILLS**

Create depth of field combining figures of varying scales.

Use techniques and materials to simulate snow, with thawing.

Take photos with realistic backgrounds and work with natural sunlight to take advantage of realistic shadows.

**SCALES**

Front figure: 1:16
Back figures: 1:35

**In recent years** I have devoted many hours to finding creative ways to execute the concept expressed in this book's title, combining scales to create realistic dioramas. The goal is always to shoot photos with great depth of field that communicate realism to the viewer. You'll find that in the projects selected here.

I start by initially taking photos of the objects I plan to use, whether figures, vegetation, or vehicles, such as airplanes, boats, or ships.

Two recent builds revolved around World War II's Battle of the Bulge in the Ardennes. The first of these dioramas presents U.S. troops. For this scene I planned for an abandoned farm, a soldier in the foreground next to an old twisted tree without leaves (obviously winter as the battle occurred during one of Europe's harshest winters), and a group of soldiers who are part of the detachment.

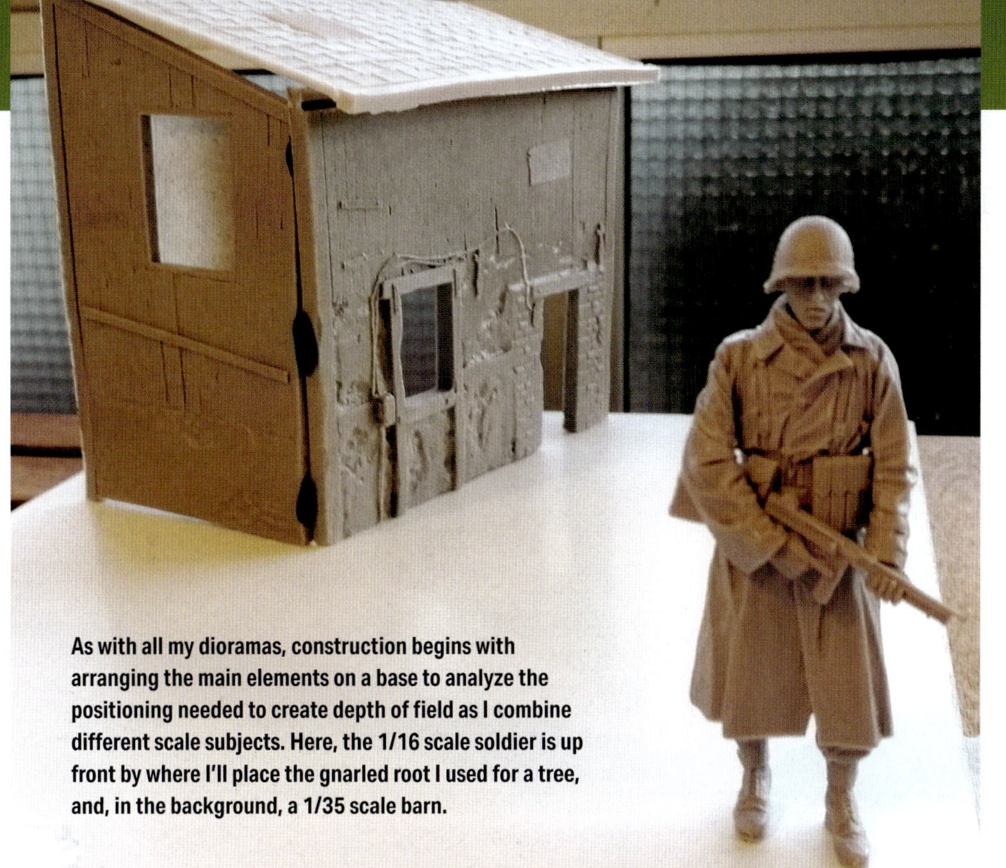

As with all my dioramas, construction begins with arranging the main elements on a base to analyze the positioning needed to create depth of field as I combine different scale subjects. Here, the 1/16 scale soldier is up front by where I'll place the gnarled root I used for a tree, and, in the background, a 1/35 scale barn.

## Diorama's story

The sequence speaks for itself: a small patrol of three combatants, dressed in coats and scarves to overcome the cold, little by little inspecting the terrain, taking great care not to run into German soldiers. While one of the American soldiers has advanced (with a lot of distrust if you look at his facial expression) the other two finish checking the interior of an abandoned barn and leave it to continue with the mission. Meanwhile, a column of armored cars (not depicted) has been gaining ground on the troops.

## Assembly, painting of American soldier

The selected 1/16 figure (No. 16022) is marketed by Alpine Miniatures. The detail is high quality and assembly simple and precise. There are barely 10 pieces to be glued: arms, boots, weapon, accessories such as a pistol, canteen, etc., and a head that comes with two possible helmets, a standard helmet or one with mesh for camouflage. I chose the latter.

There is little putty work needed, just a little on the left arm for which I use Tamiya Blue Putty dissolved in nail polish remover. Next, apply primer to the entire figure and after it dries, paint with Humbrol enamel, Mate 93, a color similar to khaki. **(1, 2)**

After it dries I paint the coat using Vallejo colors, which I use throughout the diorama, except where noted.

Here I use a variety from Khaki, (No. 70.988) to Green-Gray (No. 70.886) to Olive Green (No. 70.894) that blend well. Since this is a large figure I add oil pigments, which have the advantage of taking a long time to dry. That means you can mix different shades to bring out highlights and shadows, emphasizing areas you want accentuated. I use Pebeo pigments, but other brands will work.

Here I mix dark green, dark brown, white and lemon yellow in similar proportions to achieve a suitable tone for a weathered overcoat.

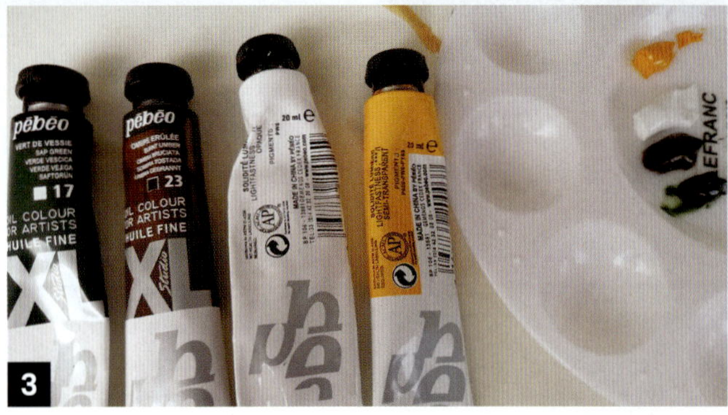


3

4

5

To create believable U.S. soldier outerwear requires creating contrasts in the soldier's coat to simulate shadows and movement. To help this I occasionally dry-brushed with Light Gray (No. 70.993) on the coat's edges and creases.

I use this mixed tone as a base for the entire coat, gradually highlighting the lights and shadows by mixing the base tone with white or black. Mixing in white gives you a shade for surface areas that you want to be lighter while adding black to the base works to create shadowy areas.

As much as I like the oil pigments I only recommend using them on large figures as the texture is thick. So with small figures the pigments could obscure details. **(3-5)**

Wait at least 72 hours for oil pigments to dry (perhaps the main disadvantage of working with them). Next, I detailed the soldier's equipment, ammunition belts, canteen, etc. with Khaki and Iraqi Sand (No. 70.819).

Lastly I focused on enhancing the accessories and details, taking advantage of the fact that this figure is large, so it allows you to work comfortably. To mark some darker parts and make a natural outlining of the coat's shadows, I use a heavily diluted mixture of Black (No. 70.950) and Green-Gray. **(6, 7)**

6

7

I also wanted to give the soldier's face an air of gloom and distrust, highlighted by his vague gaze. I followed the palette recommended by artist Jaume Ortiz in the eight-color Vallejo Face Painting set (No. 70.119), working with glazes (well-diluted acrylics) to create a play of light and shadow. Apply these little by little with a very fine brush. The set includes Beige Red (No. 70.804), Violet Red (No. 70.812), Toasted Red (No. 70.814), Base Flesh (No. 70.815), Black Red (No. 70.859), Brown Sand (No. 70.876), Pale Flesh (No. 70.928), and Black.

The weapon's metal can be painted in two ways. Either cover it with matte black and then rub with graphite powder, or paint with Gun Metal (No. 70.863) and follow by dry-brushing with Silver (No. 70.997).

8

## The old barn

The 1/35 scale old barn (No. 35256) is cast in resin by Reality in Scale and has proper detail for use in any WWII diorama. First, separate the pieces and check their condition. **(8)** This is fairly clean, needing only some minor burrs trimmed and corners filed. Note that resin models often come with slight deformations. Here I needed to correct a few gaps with putty while attaching the walls and the roof.

For assembly I used various adhesives such as superglue (instant drying), white glue (to stick the broken glass to the window) and Tamiya's two-part Epoxy Putty. That's great for sealing gaps and gluing the walls together. **(9-13)**

Assembly is simple as the kit does not contain many parts. However, it is necessary to use a bit of the epoxy putty not only to fill gaps, but also to ensure a stronger and longer-lasting bond. Small pieces, such as the wooden window, can be affixed with superglue, while other elements, such as that window's broken glass, must be attached with white glue to avoid vapors that can tarnish the transparent effect by fogging the glass.

When I glued the last wall, I found a considerable gap that had to be covered with a more versatile and softer substance than epoxy putty, so I used flexible wood putty. That's commonly used to fill flaws in woodwork or fix furniture. It dries quickly and is simple to use. Another benefit, it can be sanded easily.

9

10

11

12

13

## Abandoned barn painting and wear

Painting required patience so as not to obscure the kit's original details and texture. To imitate wood I started with a base of Cork Brown (No. 70.843). Next, I painted details, such as the upper storage door, in Khaki. Note that the chromatic tones applied early on will end up being distorted as the wear and aging process progresses. This reflects the deterioration caused by disuse and the vicissitudes of war. **(14-16)**

Next I moved on to painting the roof with Light Blue Gray (No. 70.905) with some shades for the wood to simulate old wood. These touches were made with Ochre Brown (No. 70.856) and Beige Brown (No. 70.875 from the Panzer Series). The walls were painted with Iraqi Sand and the brick areas with Red-Brown (No. 70.982), while I used different shades of gray on the tiles. Finally, I applied a highly diluted black wash and, once the roof was dry, gently dry-brushed with Light Gray. **(17-19)**

You can see most of the finished barn with all its details on the next page. **(20)**

The last of the details includes creating a rusty hatch, with Chocolate Brown (No. 70.872) and fine brushstrokes of Orange-Brown (No. 70.981). Other realistic details such as the door, were created by applying various browns with a dry brush, then adding silver details, such as the hinges and a round door knocker.

14

15

16

17

18

19

The original kit is finely detailed, which makes achieving fine wear and detailing effects much easier. Use a dry brush for adding a black wash to the barn's exterior.

20

Then I turned my attention to the brick wall, which required using various shades of reds and pinks before working on the broken glass in the window. That was cut into a jagged shape before dry-brushing its edges with white paint. Finally, highlights were applied using a variety of pastel pencils. **(20)**

The two soldiers who have been left behind the patrol, and are just leaving the barn, are slightly altered Verlinden figures that my friend Javier Labory gave me after rummaging through his spares drawer. I had to redo their paint scheme, add details, shading, and equipment. In some cases I even had to replace the original head with a new one. For the new head I used one from Verlinden's 1/35 Academy Figures Male Nude Human Body (No. 759).

Next, I painted the coats Medium Green (No. 71.092), and that same color mixed with white for the lighter accented areas. The straps and equipment are Buff (No. 70.976). Fleshy parts of the faces and hands follow the pattern used for the diorama's large figure and described earlier. To create the shadows I used diluted Black Glaze (No. 70.855), which helps achieve a realistic chiaroscuro effect. **(21-26)**

For buttons, buckles and other metal bits I used a fine silver marker like you can find in hobby and art supply stores. For the second figure I followed similar color patterns. Both helmets are painted Olive Drab (No. 70.967).

21

22

23

24

25

26

## BASE FABRICATION

For the base I used white insulating foam sheets because they are easy to shape into the uneven terrain needed for the scene. After reflecting on the placement of the different elements of the diorama (house, figures, tree) I decided the diorama would look best with the barn on elevated ground in the background. That required using several foam sheets to get the proper height. I then cut them into the right proportions and glued them to a wooden base with white glue. **(27-29)**

To carve the foam into the uneven ground needed to reflect the rough snowy surface I used an electric foam cutter. **(30)** These come in various shapes and sizes. I then prepared the area where the barn was to be placed by using a flat iron. The barn was attached with white glue. **(31, 32)**

27 28 29 30 31 32

33

34

35

Next, I added white Das putty, which dries quickly, and inserted gray pebbles that can be purchased at a hobby shop or model train store. **(33, 34)** Where needed, items were attached with more white glue, plus additional pebbles and dry branches were put in place along with the large tree that appears in the diorama's foreground. I like using natural details when possible and I had to search a wide field before finding the thick root that became the gnarled tree. Press all the trees and random branches into the foam before adding more putty and white glue to hold them in place. **(35)**

Another trick I've learned is creating additional dry branches by cutting bristles off a thick old paint brush. When inserted vertically in the foam they appear to signify that a stream is nearby. Once cut, the bristles are glued at their base while holding them tight with a finger and placing them randomly to create a sense of nature's randomness. You can cut the bristles to varying lengths to increase realism. **(36-38)**

I also added a few odds and ends to the scene's left, near the barn. This includes broken and rusted fuel drums and a shattered ladder that I made from balsa wood.

With all this in place, I used an airbrush to apply Cork Brown, then a generous layer of well-diluted Chocolate Brown around the rocks and portions of the ground. With the whole set completely dry I dry-brushed Light Blue Gray and Dark Sand (No. 70.847) around the edges of pebbles and dry branches. This creates more depth to the ground elements, aiding realism in the final scene. **(39)**

That's not all though. I then added artificial lichens, artificial grass and fragments of simulated ice. **(40)** Those are just bits of rock salt and ultraviolet resin that have been left over from making icicles for the barn's roof.

Now it's time to add snow to finish the base before gluing the figures in place.

You'll want to apply several layers of artificial snow that can look like both ice and powdery snow. This requires creating a paste made by mixing artificial Green Stuff World powder snow (Terrain Series/Snow Flock) with Transparent Gel (Still Waters) from Vallejo. **(41)**

Another option is to add Vallejo Transparent Dense Gel to the mix, depending on the texture you desire.

41

42

43

When applying the paste to simulate sleet, or a snowy terrain that is beginning to melt, use a thick brush for the terrain, and a spoon to place paste on branches and trees.

44

I recommend this paste to produce a sleet, or icy snow effect. This is particularly good for simulating a snowy terrain that is already beginning to thaw. However, due to its thickness and difficulty of application, I would not recommend this for dioramas with large snow spreads. For those, perhaps mixed white powder (plaster or similar), with water, is more appropriate.

Once the snow layer was dry, I added Talens gloss varnish, which is ideal for acrylics. This is also good for creating those icicles on the barn roof. **(42-44)**

45

## BARN ROOF ICICLES

To make the barn roof icicles I used transparent ultraviolet (UV) resin from Green Stuff World. This special resin should only be used for small visual effects, never for large artificial water surfaces. Handle it with care and always wear a mask to protect yourself from its fumes. Pour just a few drops on the desired area, then direct a beam from a UV flashlight (Green Stuff sells one) on that point. The resin dries in just seconds. (45, 46)

46

## CHAPTER THREE

**SKILLS**

Position the vehicle and aircraft at an exact distance needed to achieve depth of field in a photo with both objects being in focus.

Make realistic mud.

Adapt the position and gaze of the soldiers to look at the plane.

**SCALES**

Vehicle/figures: 1/35
Plane: 1/72

PART 2

# Tension in the Ardennes

**This second installment** of my Battle of the Bulge diorama series would involve armor and aircraft of differing scales. I wanted to create an interaction between several German soldiers on a moving vehicle, but with another element in the background presented on a different scale and the idea arose spontaneously after I asked myself two questions.

Why not an airplane? And, to make the diorama a bit more challenging, why not have the soldiers on the vehicle looking toward the sky as a fighter-bomber passes by?

My online search began with locating the classic 1/35 scale Tamiya German Flak Crew (No. 35094) which is the crew made for Tamiya's 1/35 German 8-ton half-track Sdmfz 7/1 model kit (No. 35050) that is similar to the truck I was planning to use. This crew comes in winter uniforms, so was perfect for the diorama. I would only need to modify their postures so that they could sit safely on what would appear as a moving vehicle.

But I already had an important advantage, most of these figures already are looking toward the sky because they are intended to be manning the half-track's anti-aircraft gun.

## AB43 CONSTRUCTION AND PAINTING

After locating the crew I turned my attention to the vehicle I'd pose at the front of the diorama. I had to be sure to use a vehicle present at the battle, and my online detective work confirmed the German AB43 203 armored car would work. That was fortunate because I already had an assembled Tamiya version (No. 89697) that I'd found in a box of old models I had at home. Some parts already had been painted and some parts were missing, so I had to repaint and fix a few details.

First I checked all the joints to assure the model was sturdy, then went over the model with sandpaper and removed excess dust and grime. Next I superglued on the missing parts and added other details. I had to fabricate, using sheet styrene, part of the turret's top hatch.

Finally I went back to do a general check of the pieces to assure nothing was missing before moving on to the painting. **(1-5)**

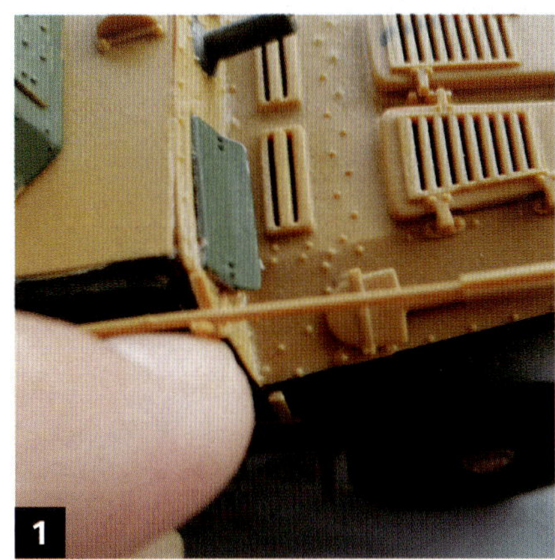
1

2

3

4

5

Before the final painting and adding wear I attached additional accessories such as a miniature chain to the vehicle's front wheels. Let the wash dry for at least one night.

**ADDING WINTER WEAR AND TEAR**

Using a dry brush is vital to emphasize the vehicle's textures, both for the armor's bolts, and to enhance the mud's roughness.

To emphasize the wear on the armor use a sharp No. 10 hobby blade to chip at the surface.

I started by applying a base of Tamiya Dark Yellow (XF-88) which is the base color for German tanks from 1943. After allowing it to dry for 24 hours, I applied a thin dark brown wash using Citadel's Agrax Earthshade ink. Be sure the wash is very thin so the bolts and other vehicle details show through. **(6-8)**

## Creating winter camo and mud

As documented in various bibliographical sources, the winter camouflage of German vehicles was applied directly to the Dark Yellow base with layers and strokes of white paint visible over the base.

This effect can be achieved by using diluted white paint and old brushes with deteriorated and open bristles. I tried to leave some small areas where you can see that Dark Yellow under the white. In this case the yellow layer was thick enough to allow chipping afterward with a sharp No. 10 hobby blade. This represents typical battle damage to the armor. **(9)**

To increase the vehicle's realism in the scene, I also:

- Added wear to the decals.
- Used an airbrush to spray a mixture of water, a few drops of Mig Ultra-Matt Lucky Varnish (AMIG 2050, an acrylic-based varnish), and a few drops of Vallejo Black (No. 70.950). Again note that I primarily use Vallejo paints, unless otherwise stated.
- Dry-brushed Pure White (No. 70.951) on the edges and screws.

To simulate mud on the wheels I prepared a paste of Real Dark Earth Gel (26.218), attaching it with transparent silicone glue using a brush. Once it was dry I used a dry brush to highlight the texture with Chocolate Brown (No. 70.872) and white.

## The figures

Experienced modelers know the pleasure of working with a Tamiya kit because of the parts fit, precision, and scale fidelity. The German halftrack crew was no exception as I adapted it to fit the diorama's action. But of course I was going to need to rearrange some of the crew's body parts before detailing their winter uniforms.

With tools such as a mini-saw, pliers, etc., I worked with almost all the figures at the same time, removing legs, trunks, arms, and heads, then combining their different positions to create realistic figures that could sit on the vehicle and look overhead at the airplane.

The set contained five figures, and I ended up using four, three to place on the vehicle, and a driver. I had decided to open the front hatch to show the driver's gaze to create further interest. Prior to painting, the preliminary work consisted of two important processes: dissolving Tamiya Putty in nail polish remover to cover small gaps that were left when placing the arms and legs (the figures had to be credibly holding on to the vehicle to avoid falling off when it was moving), and model small pieces of two-component Tamiya Epoxy Putty to make necessary extensions while adapting the figures' postures. **(10-13)**

10

11

12

13

14

15

16

**Here you can we see how practical it is to finish some details with a brush after the figures are already attached. This is also the time to highlight details and add light accents by using pastel pencils. That's exactly what I did with the driver in place. I could see that adding a dab of sunlight to his face would add more realism.**

Painting the reversible uniforms (camouflage and white) was not difficult as the colors are explained well on the figure kit's box. But painting the faces takes time and patience. I started with a layer of Basic Skin (No. 70.815), and continuing with the eyes, outlining the upper lid with black before adding the pupil. Lastly I turned to the lips (mixing Basic Skin with a bit of Cavalry Brown (No. 70.982) and finishing with a well-diluted wash of Burnt Red (No. 70.814). **(14)**

To create the lived-in look, the white winter uniforms should be slightly darkened with a wash of well-diluted black paint.

Once painted and dry, the figures were test-fit on the vehicle. First they had to be positioned to check that their poses were natural. **(15)**

The soldiers would ride up front and on top with the officer in the turret hatch. But I had to take a few photos to make sure their positions did not look forced. **(17)**

Here's what I took into account.

1. That they kept their gazes skyward and slightly to their right
2. That they clung to some physical point on the AB43.
3. That each soldier carried his regulation weapon. Before gluing the vehicle's turret in its final position, I opened the front hatch a little more and put the driver in position. **(16)**

## ADDING FINAL DETAILS

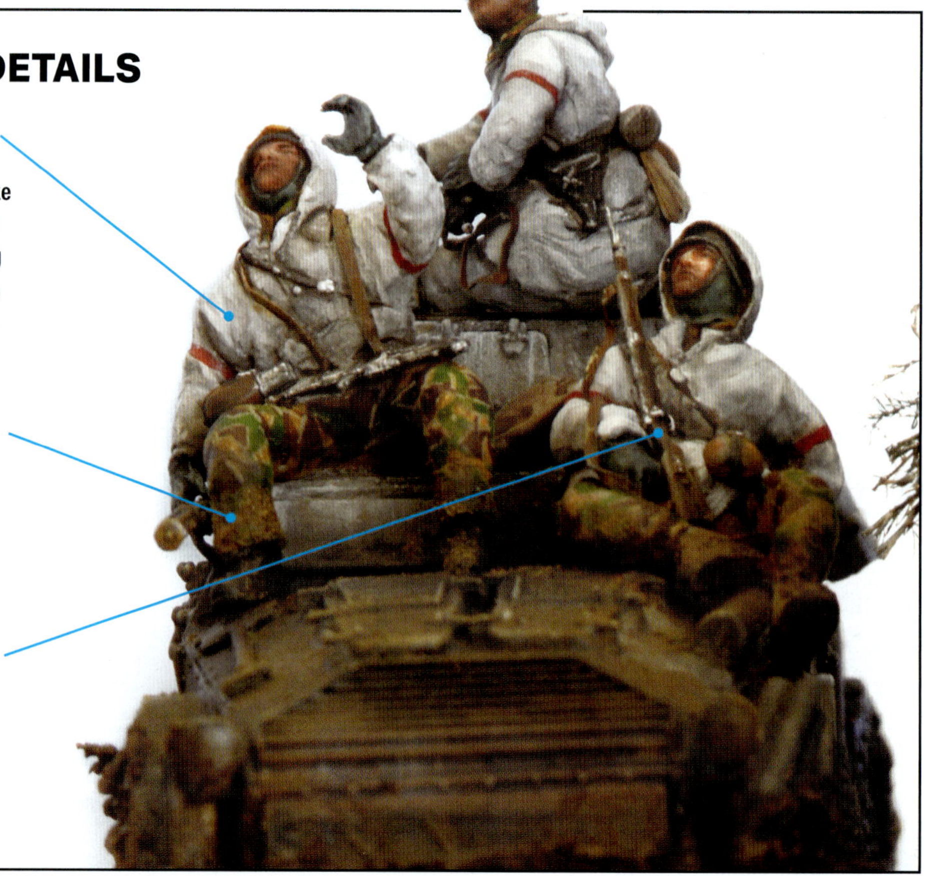

**The soldiers' winter uniforms are white, but shaded with grays and blacks. But the key here was to make sure they were gazing skyward and slightly to the right, that they clung to the vehicle with at least one arm, and that they all carried regulation weapons and belts.**

**It's important to highlight the dirt created by mud, both on the legs and lower portions of the soldiers' uniforms, and where they have stepped on the vehicle.**

**Once the figures are in place it's time to paint and add final details, such as the soldiers' equipment, weapons, and belt buckles, which are made of tinfoil.**

17

## The aircraft

Next, I turned my attention skyward.

I had chosen the 1/72 scale Focke-Wulf Fw 190D-9 by Tamiya (No. 61041). In addition to its fine detail, the kit includes a version of decals and paint that was historically compatible with my Ardennes scene, which represents the morning of Jan. 1, 1945. On that date this AB43 passes by a muddy path next to snow-laden fir trees when suddenly a light bomber appears overhead. The Fw 190D-9 was one of the most used planes by the Luftwaffe during World War II.

In the scene, the plane soars into the sky after carrying out an attack during Operation Bodenplatte, the German offensive aimed at supporting its troops in the Battle of the Ardennes. Operation Bodenplatte was an attempt to destroy Allied aviation in Belgium, but it failed. This was the last German air offensive during WWII.

The unopened model came to me from my friend Secundino Elías Darias García, who has advised me on aviation history of this period. Fit was perfect, which made for a quick, easy build, with little need for a file or putty. The build started with the cockpit and painting the figure. **(18, 19)**

Little by little I added wings, fuselage and landing gear, trying not to leave any glue stains. I used Tamiya's Extra Thin liquid cement because it's

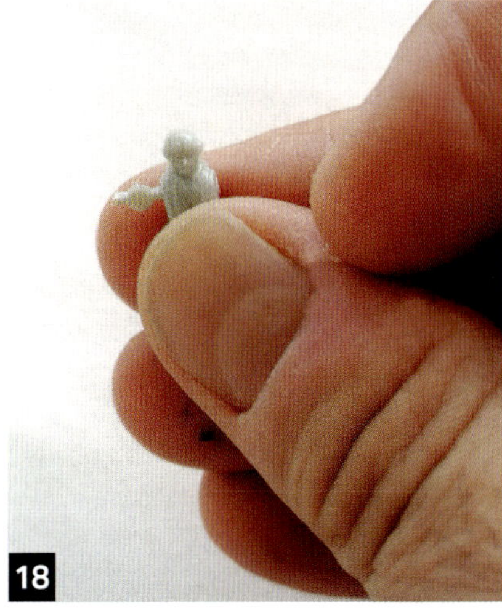

18

19

20

21

22

23

Painting left me with this fabulous Fw 190D-9 that was created by airbrushing the upper aircraft with German Camouflage Bright Green (No. 70.833), and German Gray (No. 70.995). Then the model was treated to a wash of Black Glaze (No. 70.855) and dry brushing with Pale Gray Blue (No. 70.907) and then fine lines applied with a light gray pastel pencil. The streaking effect on the wings creates the illusion of speed, helping bring action to the diorama. Other wear came from using Tamiya Weathering Master sets. These look a bit like makeup cases, but with colored pastel powders to help simulate dirt and other weathering effects.

24

clean and easy to use while avoiding excess cement oozing from joins.

Originally I intended to leave the landing gear open, but decided it was more logical to close them. The plane was on a bombing mission and would not be landing anytime soon. **(20-23)**

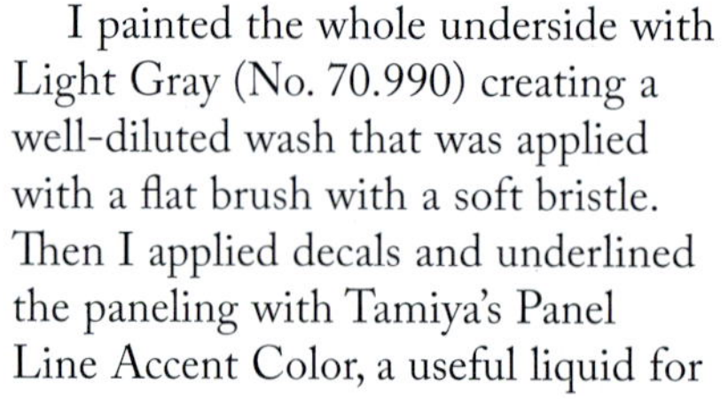

I painted the whole underside with Light Gray (No. 70.990) creating a well-diluted wash that was applied with a flat brush with a soft bristle. Then I applied decals and underlined the paneling with Tamiya's Panel Line Accent Color, a useful liquid for creating effects of dirt, wear, shadow and oil stains on airplanes. **(24)**

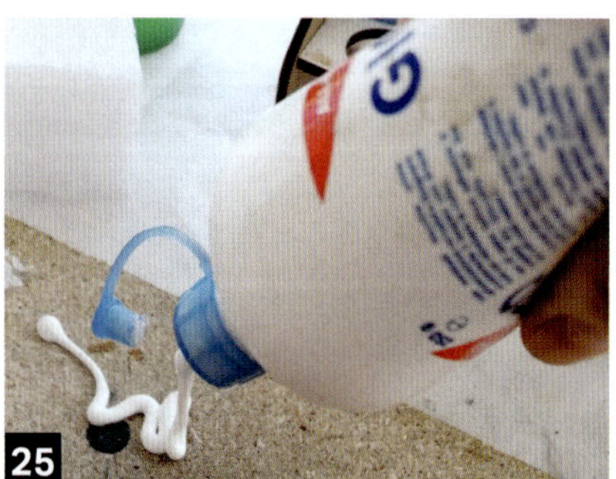

25

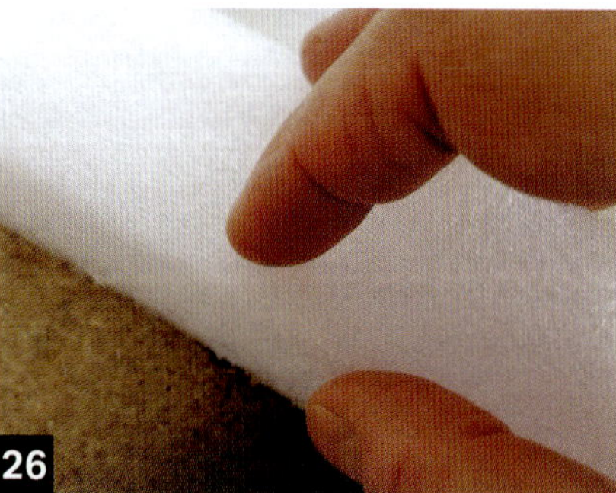

26

27

## Assembling the diorama

The approach to this scene was simple: place a vehicle on a rural road flanked by trees laden with snow and suspend a plane on a wire to create a realistic photographic simulation. The Battle of the Bulge took place during a bitterly cold and snowy winter, so that had to be re-created with heavy snow on the ground and trees to set the proper tone. Research shows that hail was a major factor too, so pines were especially thickly coated.

For this I used Aguaplast, a type of plaster sold in hardware stores and used to cover holes in walls. Aguaplast is sold already prepared, presenting a texture similar to yogurt, or in a powder form to be mixed with water, in varying proportions. That's what I used to create the snowy covering for the trees. Both types generally dry quickly, overnight at the longest.

First, I prepared two sheets of foam

28

29

30

insulation, using white glue to attach them to a fiberboard base, establishing the initial position of the path running through the center of the diorama. I was careful to assure the path was wide enough so that the vehicle could be placed comfortably for photo purposes. Next, with a pyrograph (wood-burning tool), I carved the foam's edges to form natural slopes in the terrain. **(25-27)**

Once the foam was firmly in place I covered the ground with the semi-liquid version of Aguaplast because it's easily applied with a spatula. That yogurt-type consistency allows it to reach all the nooks and crannies of the foam-based terrain. **(28, 29)**

With the same spatula I prepared the path's surface and then used pieces of chain, extra model truck wheels and tracks to easily simulate a variety of tracks and marks on the snowy ground. **(30)** Once the Aguaplast was dry I checked to make sure the vehicle properly fit into the diorama. **(31)**

Next, I prepared the tree trunks that would simulate snowy pines. I cut a few leftover twigs from a small log that I'd found before making holes with a mini-drill on all sides of the bigger branch that I was using for the trunk. I spaced these about 2 inches apart. **(32, 33)**

I've found the best natural vegetation to simulate pine branches is asparagus, often easily found in summer. The problem with this shrub

31

32

33

34

35

is that, once cut to meet our modeling purposes, it must be treated gently as the twigs and foliage become delicate. It's easy for its fine leaves to be damaged or fall off just by handling it. To help avoid this, I spray freshly cut asparagus with a matte varnish and various shades of green paint. This helps delay the twigs from shedding their foliage.

Once they were stabilized I placed the trees around the diorama, attaching them with white glue and Das white putty. **(34, 35)**

For the background I used smaller scale artificial pine trees from one of the various hobby brands. This simulated the depth of field I needed. Then I used an airbrush to apply a first coat of Yellow Ochre (No. 70.913) to the path and ground cover.

Finally I coated the ground with a wash of Burnt Umber (No. 70.941) to create a muddy texture for under the snow, insinuating daytime thawing and melting. **(36, 37)**

Next, I covered the trees with snow. To simulate snow accumulation on the pines' crowns I turned to Aguaplast powder (Ratioplast brand). I like using the powder, which is mixed with water to create the consistency you desire, because it's easy to adjust. Then brush the fake snow into the canopy of pine trees you've created. Be gentle so as not to break the twigs that are acting as branches. **(38, 39)**

Before attaching the vehicle permanently I applied a generous coat of artificial Thick Mud—European Mud (No. 26.807). This makes the sloppy path more believable. **(40, 41)** I then glued the vehicle in place before adding mud to its wheels with a small stick so it looks to be moving through the muck.

Once the mud dried, I reinforced its fresh nature by adding small amounts of artificial Water Texture Still Waters (No. 26.230). **(42)**

Finished! **(43)**

36

37

38

39

40

41

42

43 Here we see a detail of the mud as it oozes off the tires, indicating visually that the vehicle is moving.

## CHAPTER FOUR

# George Washington crossing the Delaware River

**SKILLS**

Work from scratch with figures to achieve poses similar to those in the painting.

Create an icy river and winter atmosphere.

Place three scales in position to re-create a realistic background.

**SCALES**

Washington's boat: 1:32
Second boat: 1:56
Third boat: 1:72

Emanuel Gottlieb Leutze. Washington Crossing the Delaware. 1851. Metropolitan Museum of Art. Wikimedia Commons.

**This diorama** was undoubtedly the most complex due to the number of figures included (30) and the difficulty of adapting the positions of the combatants to reflect those in the famous Emanuel Leutze painting, *Washington Crossing the Delaware* (1851). The idea was suggested to me in 2015 by a friend and colleague José María López Lago, born in Chicago, whom I thank for his conviction to creating this dramatic historical diorama.

Gen. George Washington's crossing of the Delaware River during the American Revolutionary War was a historic military turning point. It famously took place on Christmas night and the morning of Dec. 26, 1776, and was the first move in a surprise attack Washington had planned against the Hessian soldiers, commanded by Johann Rall at Trenton, N.J.

The diorama was difficult for several reasons. First, to achieve a realistic representation of Leutze's painting I had to work from scratch, or semi-scratch, to re-create the painting's main figures. That entailed assembling and painting some of the figures two or three times, working with various heads, torsos, arms, and legs, all from various manufacturers. Those included Andrea Miniatures, Latorre Models, LOD Enterprises, Hornet, TMP, Revell, Preiser, Historex, BUM, Art Girona, Perry Miniatures, and Airfix.

But this combination meant some figures were made of parts from up to five sources. However, that meant they each had their own unique personality. It also meant I had to work with different putties, tinfoil, and other materials to complete their uniforms and accessorize the scene.

1

2

3

## Phase I: 1/72 scale boat, crew

With three boats and crews to make, one each in the various scales, I started by buying the hard-to-find BUM (Barcelona Universal Models) 1/72 scale kit, Washington Delaware (No. 2255). It includes a resin boat and crew with acceptable detail, but needed paint work and aging.

As with my other builds, I primarily used Vallejo finishing products, unless otherwise noted. First I painted the whole set a medium brown, Tierra (No. 70.873). I followed that with a coat of liquid acrylic retarder (Royal Talens 070) to help give the boat's wood an aged look. I then applied some greens, ochre, and grays. To complete the process, I dry-brushed with Sand Yellow (No. 69.033) and made careful touches with a tile-colored pastel pencil. **(1-4)**

To man the boat I selected figures from Revell's American War of Independence series, specifically, American Militia and British Infantry, whose uniforms were similar to America's militia. **(5, 6)** The paint scheme on all the 1/72 figures was a Dark Blue uniform (No. 70.925), White straps (No. 70.951), and Black boots (No. 70.950) for the Colonial army, and Flat Brown (No. 70.984), Blue Gray Pale (No. 70.905), and Flat Green (No. 70.968) for militia units. I used Flat Flesh (No. 70.955) for faces, darkened with Vallejo Game Color Flesh Wash (No. 73.204).

As these are extremely small figures, they had to adapt to the space when being positioned in the boat. Because the space was so tight I finished painting the figures once they were glued in place. **(7)** When I later placed the gun in the boat a few figures had to be removed. **(8)**

To paint details in such tight spaces use very fine brushes, double zero or triple zero will work. Also No. 1 and No. 2 brushes with a thin top can be used.

4

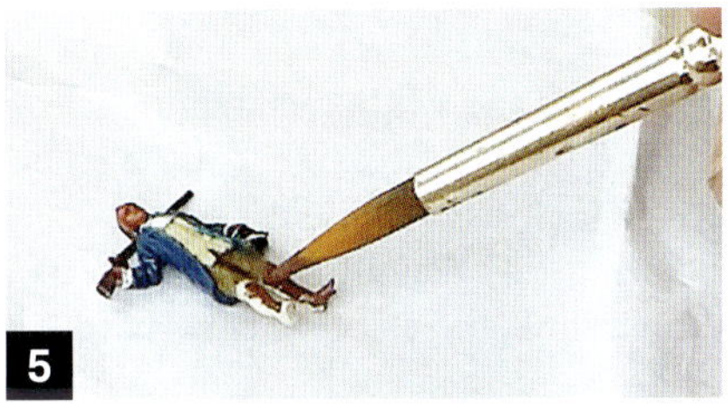

5

6

7

8

## Phase II: 1/56 scale boat, crew

To really make this diorama work I needed an intermediate scale, 1/56, for the middle boat, and luckily TMP made just that, a kit called Washington Crossing the Delaware. It includes a resin boat and white metal figures. I needed more figures to adapt the scene to more closely represent Leutze's painting, so I bought more from Perry Miniatures. The color scheme that I followed to decorate the figures, in this case, was the same as the one used for the boat and the previous 1/72 scale crew. **(9-11)**

I was more careful with the details here since, working at this scale, the viewer, and camera, would likely notice more as it is closer to the main focus of the diorama and would be closer to the camera. Although both the middle and rear boats were to essentially be part of the background, this needed more detail, so I used fine wire to achieve more realism in the oars and poles that the soldiers used to move blocks of ice in the river.

I also had to use balsa strips to extend the boat's length to make it more like what Leutze's painting depicts. Again I used Flat Brown on the boat and aged it with a dark brown wash. As before, I painted many of the figures once they were glued inside the boat, for example the soldier sitting in the boat's bow with a blanket. **(13-16)**

I made the horses' manes with cotton soaked in paint to try to imitate the wind's movement. I also had to add small wooden slats and increase the boat's length for visual purposes.

14

15

16

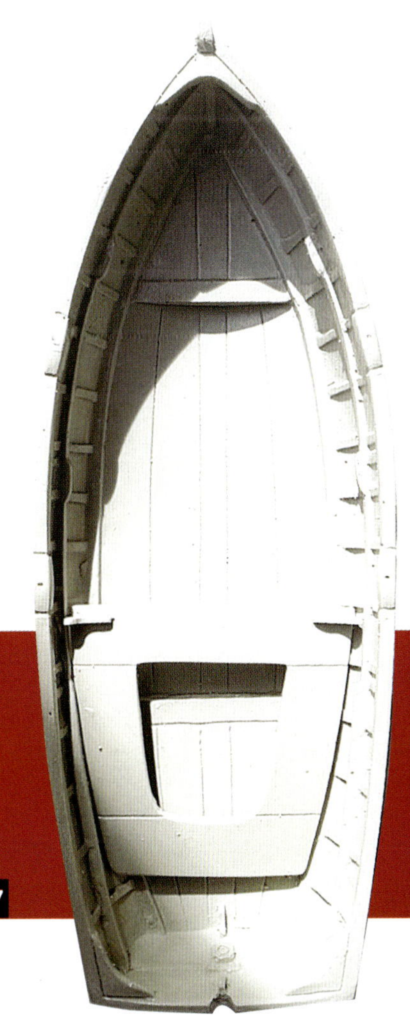
17

### Phase III: 1/24 scale boat, 1/32 scale crew

Here's where things became interesting and more complex, especially in finding a boat and creating the figures.

First I found a balsa wood boat, but it was too large to fit the scene. Second was a 1/35 model that was too small to hold the 12 figures I needed to squeeze in. Third time was the charm, a 1/24 resin model from The Model Dockyard. **(17)** This was the Quaycraft 14-foot Clinker Dinghy Transom Stern (No. QD24).

18

19

20

21

22

23

24

## Painting the big boat

My first smart move was gluing the boat to a piece of wood to steady it, allowing me to paint it more comfortably. I began by applying a base coat of Earth Brown (No. 71.136), making sure that it dried with a flat finish. To bring out the nooks and crannies in the wood, I applied a wash of Citadel Agrax Earthshade. **(18)**

Once dry, I applied a coat of acrylic retardant liquid, as on the first boat, which allows easier blending of pigments to create varying gradations and tones. **(19)**

To imitate old and worn wood, I applied diluted brushstrokes of Ochre (No. 70.856), Olive Green (No. 70.894), Dark Sand (No. 70.847) and Chocolate Brown (No. 70.872). **(20, 21)**

I generally use a plastic palette to keep colors separate, or when mixing paints.

Next, to highlight the boat's grain, I dry-brushed using Humbrol's Desert Yellow paint (Matt 93). A warning, first be sure to stir the bottom of the paint pot with a stick to fully mix the color and assure the paint dries with a flat finish. Then, moisten the brush, removing the excess paint on a cloth so that it's quite dry before dry-brushing the model. This ensures better results. **(22-24)**

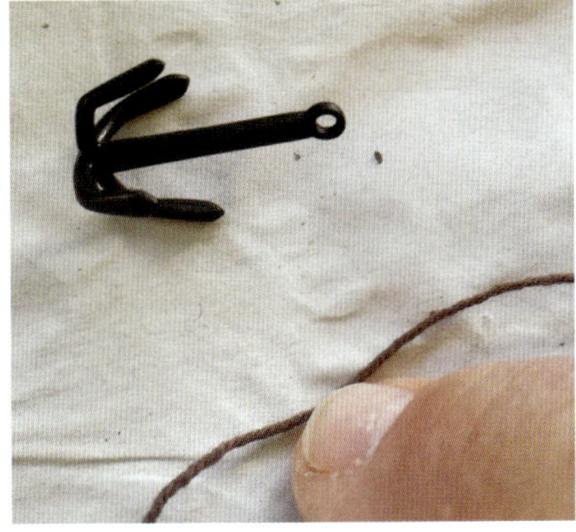

**Accessories are important**

For years people have contemplated Emanuel Leutze's painting and no doubt imagined all sorts of supplies, weapons, ammunition, and other equipment were being carried in those boats, despite their small size. Such contemplation led me to accessorize Washington's boat to further enrich the scene. I added a lantern with an extinguished candle (which I made with 22 pieces of plastic and metal and a fragment of methacrylate), a bucket, ropes, a blanket, some boxes, and a naval boat hook.

## GEORGE WASHINGTON'S CREW

To re-create Washington and his crew to resemble those in Leutze's famous painting I would have to be organized, plus study and research each figure in detail. I first verified that no model manufacturer had created these figures, which encouraged me to work with enthusiasm and patience to create a unique diorama. I was aware that I would have to work with various figures (more than 20) and bits and pieces from a wide variety of manufacturers. This would cost a lot of money, but then this was going to be a special scene.

Leutze's figures were represented in foreshortened poses, inspired by the tension of war, and full of dynamic movement. Their faces were empathetic and reflected the psychological moment before the attack.

There also was the partially unfurled American flag and he emphasized the winter atmosphere with snow and dramatic ice blocks clogging the Delaware River. To create more movement he emphasized the wind with blowing hair and billowing soldiers' scarves.

I organized the project by numbering each figure, and then creating each one in a pose as similar as possible to those in Leutze's scene. I worked slowly and patiently to take advantage of the space available in the boat and to let each figure show its personality and purpose. I'll individually describe how I created each figure, going from left to right (bow to stern) and in the order I numbered the 12 figures. I completed constructing and painting each figure before placing them all in the boat. I used Vallejo paints, except where noted.

**Leutze achieved great dynamism in his painting with a crew member in the bow and one in the stern rowing and pushing ice blocks aside. Here I created the front soldier by piecing together arms and legs from various figure manufacturers to replicate his stance and reforming his uniform with Milliput white putty. After painting the figure I created the fur texture of his hat using a metal brush.**

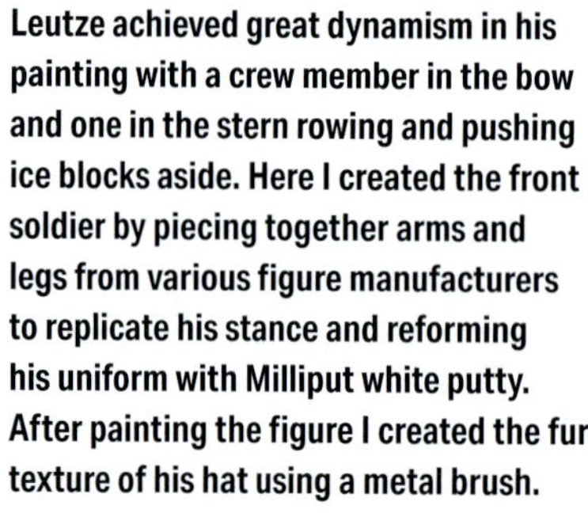

This first figure was certain to be difficult as he was balanced on the boat's bow and had to grab a long pole to move ice blocks and remove obstacles from the boat's path.

Combining several pieces of legs and arms, I shaped the figure to best reflect its overall pose. Next came the resin head from Historex. I used Milliput two-part white putty to improve the sleeve pleats and shape the hat, while using a metal brush to create the hat's furry texture. I simulated the scarf's movement with a piece of tinfoil.

Thankfully the color scheme was simple. I applied Buff (No. 70.976) for the hat, Medium Olive (No. 70.850) for the shirt, Olive Green (No. 70.967) for the pants, Vermilion (No. 70.909) for the scarf, and Black (No. 70.950) for the boots. I also used Yellow Ochre (No. 70.913) to highlight the shirt. I made the belt with a thin rope. The stick is a length of solder, stretched with two pliers to make it as straight as possible. It is painted with Chocolate Brown (No. 70.872).

I had to do several tests with the hands so that they were correctly placed. I eventually used Preiser hands of the proper scale.

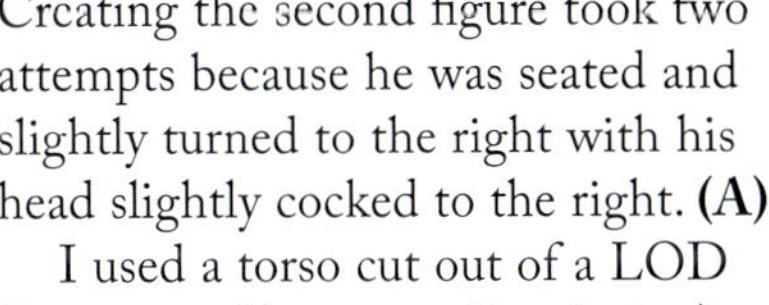

Creating the second figure took two attempts because he was seated and slightly turned to the right with his head slightly cocked to the right. **(A)**

I used a torso cut out of a LOD Enterprise (American Revolution) figure and made the oar from a piece of tin wire partially melted. Again I used Milliput putty to create the figure's hat. **(C)**

Painting involved using Light Turquoise (No. 70.840) for the hat and scarf around his neck, Vermilion (No. 70.909) for the ball atop his hat, Chocolate Brown (No. 70.872) for the jacket, Yellow Ochre (No. 70.913) and Silver (No. 70.997) for the belt, and Dark Sand (No. 70.847) for the stockings. The shoes were painted Black (No. 70.950), while Ivory (No. 70.918) was used for the shirt. I had to be especially careful painting the figure's cap as it features small red and white rectangles. **(B)**

**I finished the figure's cap by detailing it with small pieces of white Das Pronto putty and a small strip of tinfoil.**

Leutze included a multiracial crew in his painting, along with people of different nationalities and ages, plus officers and foot soldiers. Figure 3 is black. I again created him by using various model figure pieces. I was especially concerned to find a head to reflect the black soldier's physical characteristics. I found it in a 1/32 scale Preiser figure, "Adam" (No. 63900). I also was able to use the figure's arms, but found a Historex figure's legs worked better for this sitting position. **(A, B)**

To make small improvements to the clothes, I used, for this and the following figures, two-part Tamiya Epoxy Putty, which gives good results as it hardens quickly and can be molded easily using various hobby tools. The putty also allowed me to smooth clothing shapes with a water-soaked brush.

I used much of the paint from the previous figure, including Vermilion (No. 70.909) for the shirt, Chocolate Brown (No. 70.872) for the pants, Black (No. 70.950) for the boots, and Dark Blue (No. 70.930) for the jacket. Painting the hands and face was not easy. I had to choose a shade that did not obscure features. Flat Brown (No. 70.984) worked. I also used a hobby visor with a light, helpful when painting faces.

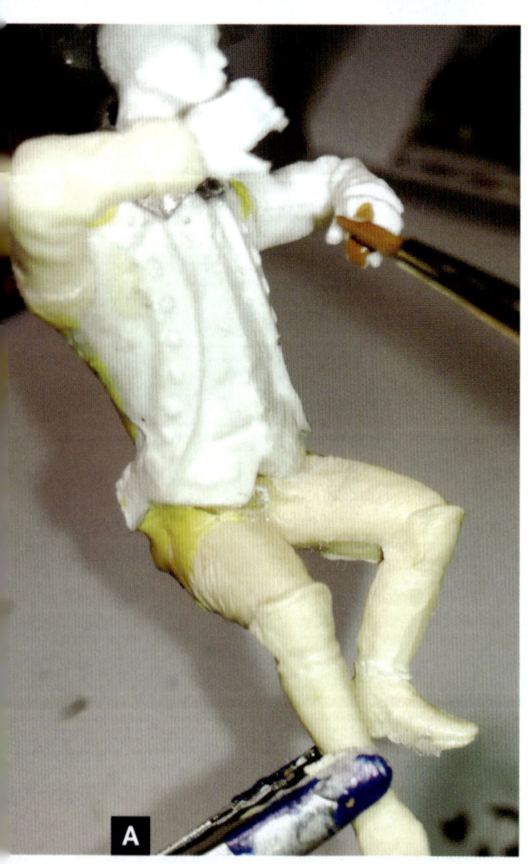

A

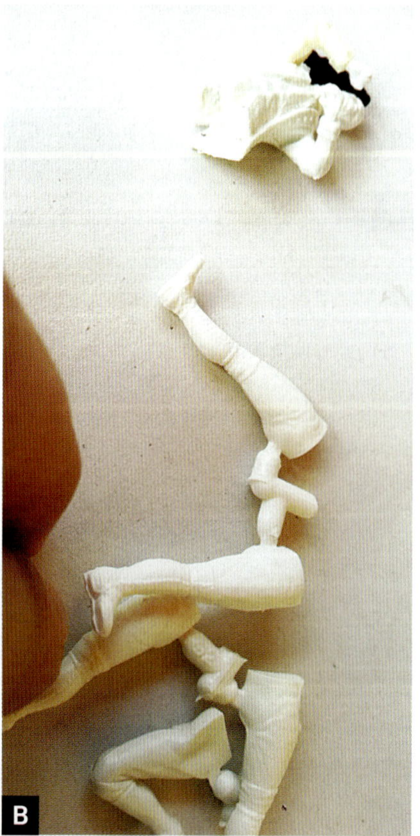

B

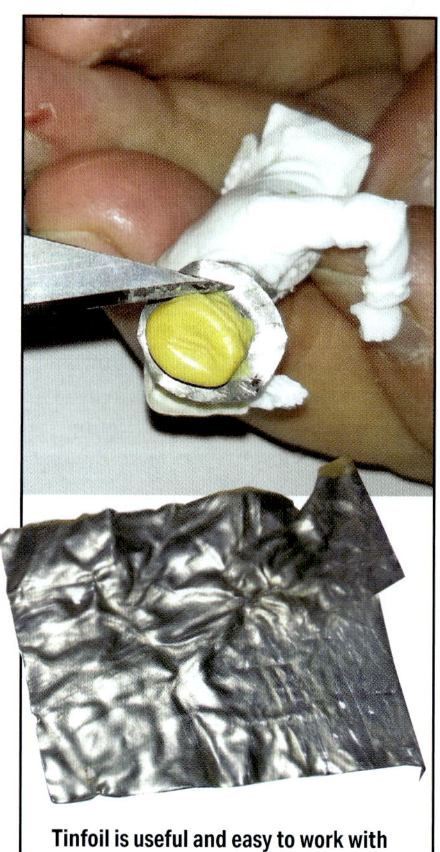

Tinfoil is useful and easy to work with while maintaining its shape. I used it to make hats, capes, and accessories for this diorama's figures.

This figure is an officer sitting next to Washington in an observation pose, leaning on the edge of the boat. He is dressed in a dark blue cape and a classic northern army cap. As with the previous figure, it was somewhat difficult to find figure pieces to create the best position, especially the legs as there was limited space in the boat. But once I did, I worked to shape the cape with white Milliput putty, and again smoothed it with a brush dipped in water. **(A, B)**

The colors were simple, using the same skin tones as in previous figures, Base Flesh (No. 70.815) with a Dark Flesh Wash (No. 73.204), and various shades of blue, including Dark Blue (No. 70.930), Prussian Blue (No. 70,899) and Fluorescent Blue (No. 70.736) for the cape's lighter areas. **(C)**

Finally, I applied highlights with a sky blue pastel pencil.

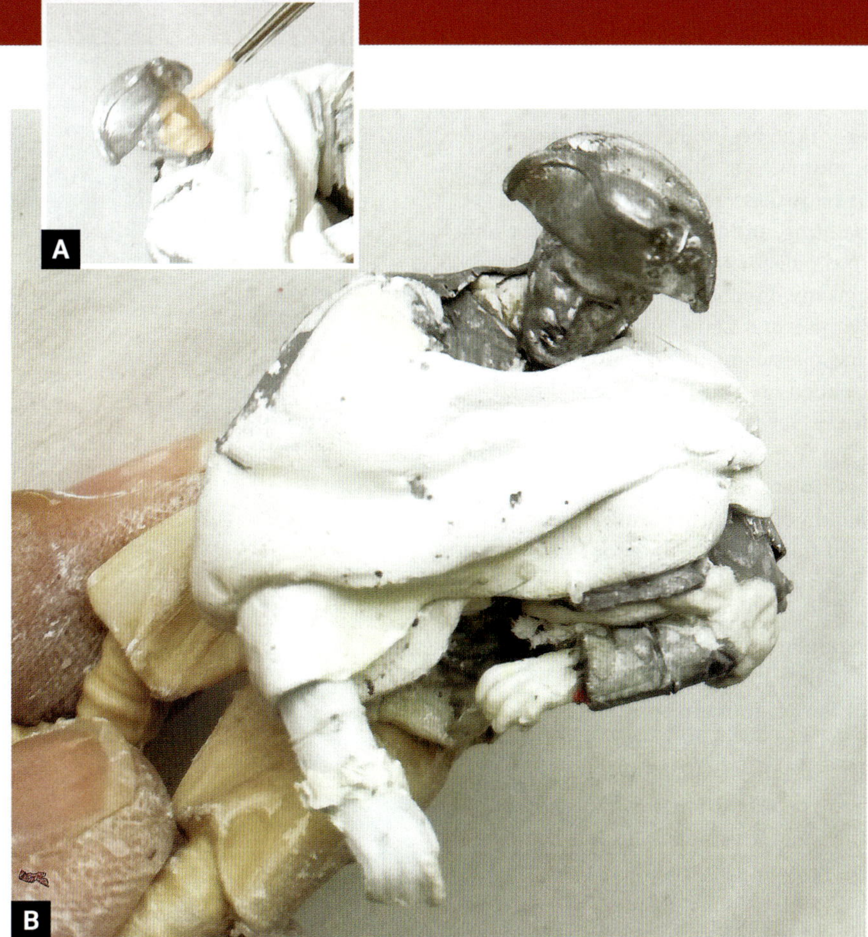

## George Washington

From the beginning I was aware of the importance of the Washington figure as he is the central figure in the Leutze painting, and the main protagonist due to the history captured in this scene, and my diorama. So I tried working with several figures, both white metal and plastic, making a couple versions. I ended up using the body and head from Der Bunte Rock's white metal Gen. Von Steuben figure (No. 54-008), and the right arm, but changed its hand position. Then I used the left arm from Airfix's figure of Washington (No. 02554-8), again altering the hand position. I sanded the metal body carefully beforehand.

Once I had the arms and hands in the appropriate positions I again used Milliput white putty and Tamiya Epoxy Putty to blend them into the body before turning my attention to the cape. It was difficult as it had to show some raised folds at the top indicating the wind's affect. This would require tinfoil trimmed to the proper size and shaped to reflect its movement.

Certainly achieving the complex folds of the cape at Washington's left hand, which grips the cape to prevent the wind from blowing it, wasn't easy. Adding further detail I got lucky, finding a sword (similar to that in Leutze's painting) in my spares box.

Washington's uniform color palette included Sky Gray (No. 70.989); Vermilion (No. 70.909) for the inside of the cape, Dark Blue (No. 70.930) for the jacket, Ochre Brown (No. 70.856) for the rest of the uniform, and Black (No. 70.950), Silver (No. 70.997) and Gold (No. 70.996) for the details.

Face painting took a bit more finesse as I also wanted his face to reflect pre-combat tension, a frown, a sharp gaze on the risky incursion's goal, a three-day beard, and the typical wig common in the 18th century. I finished by using a pastel pencil to add highlights to the figure's clothing.

Figure 5

The standard bearer is, without a doubt, the figure that occupies the painting's central position and, together with Washington, communicates with viewers. My diorama had to reflect this.

I took advantage of the fine detail of Airfix's 1/35 scale American Soldier 1776 (No. 01555-8) figure with arms in a position to hold the Betsy Ross-designed flag upright with his arms, as in the painting. There is some controversy because historical sources indicate that the first time this flag was taken into battle was in 1777, a year after the Battle of Trenton, but the painter used it to bring more solemnity to the scene, as many historians consider the Betsy Ross-designed flag as among the first official U.S. flags.

Figure 6

**The Airfix figure didn't need much work, just sanding and a bit of basic Tamiya putty dissolved in nail polish remover to fill cracks. A little Tamiya epoxy putty also was used to improve detailing before I added a tinfoil collar, cut and folded in the proper proportions, to the standard bearer's uniform.**

**Painting was similar to previous figures, with the exception of the uniform's white tone. To achieve a shadow effect on the uniform I used White (No. 70.951), then applied a soft wash of Ivory (No. 70.918).**

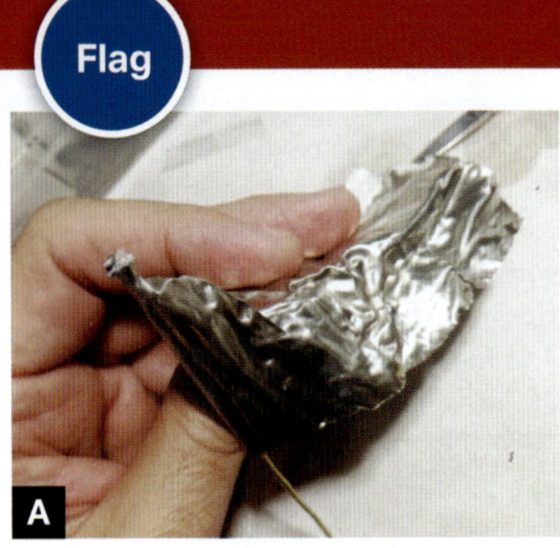
A

B

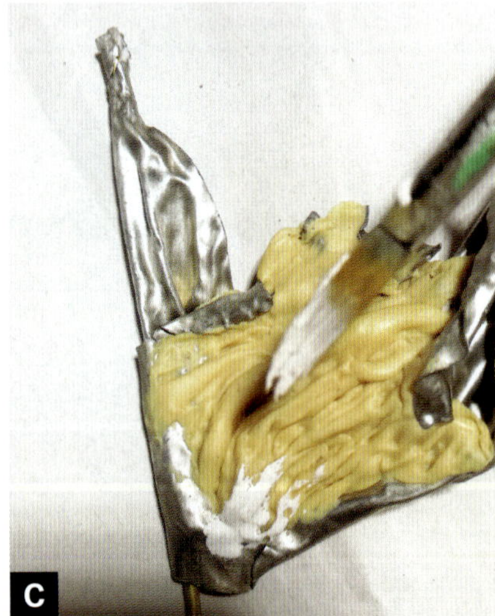
C

D

## Re-creating the flag

Making the flag took time and patience. I worked on it little by little, creating pleats from tinfoil along with small bits of Tamiya epoxy putty. To smooth those folds I used a brush dipped in water before the putty dried. **(A, B, C)**

Next I painted the flag with Vallejo Red (No. 70.926), White (No. 70.951), and Dark Blue (No. 70.930)and although I had brush-painted the stars I was not happy with the results. So I cut out stars, one by one, from a color reproduction on paper and applied them with white glue. Once they dried I applied two very diluted washes, waiting for each to dry before adding another. The first was made with Light Gray (No. 71.050), the second with Black Glaze (No. 70.855). **(D)**

Finally, to add a shadow effect I airbrushed a mix of Black, MIG matte Lucky Varnish (No. 2055) and water, with the black being very diluted. **(E)**

E

The soldier helping the standard bearer hold the flag tightly (a significant wind presence can be seen in the painting), presented another complicated, forced pose.

While his legs and torso are directed forward, his arms hold the flag. I started with a figure from Barzso's 1/32 scale Revolutionary War Colonial Minutemen set (now marketed by LOD Enterprises and easily found on the internet) as his clothing was correct with a long coat and appropriate accessories. **(A)**

I again used tinfoil to make a wide belt, and Tamiya epoxy putty to form a scarf and fur hat. Again I found a sword in my spares box, painting it with Black (No. 70.950), and Silver (No. 70.997). **(B, C)**

For the figure I used Ivory (No. 70.918) for the coat, White (No. 70.951) for the belt, Turquoise (No. 70.966) for the scarf, Earth Brown (No. 71.290) for the other belt and gunpowder horn, Black for the shoes, White for the smock and socks, and WWII Japanese Uniform Brown (No. 70.923) for the pants. I also applied washes of Brown Glaze (No. 70.854) and Black Glaze (No. 70.855) to create shadows.

**Figure 7**

A

B

C

## Painting a head

**To paint a head, first superglue it to a pencil's eraser. The pencil's lightness and ease of handling allows you to more easily paint fine details. Facial colors usually include Basic Skin (No. 70.815), eyes of black and white, with shadows added via Flesh Wash (No. 73.204). Finally I applied highlights with a pastel pencil, adding touches of sky blue to the scarf.**

Figure 8

A

B

C

This seated rowing figure brings great contrast, color and movement to the scene. His crimson shirt, similar to a brick red, is an attractive contrast to other adjoining figures' colors.

I chose a bare head from Historex, legs belonging to an Andrea Miniatures (US Revolutionary Infantryman, 1780) figure, and a torso from an Art Girona figure (Minutemen 1770-83). The pose wasn't easy. While the character's head is turned to the right, his body moves backward as he rows. **(A)**

The arms came from my spares box and I did a bit of detailing with Tamiya epoxy putty. **(B)** I also used it to create the figure's curly hair.

Next I cut out the flowing scarf from a small sheet of tinfoil, giving it a wavy shape to imitate blowing wind. **(C)** Finally I added a period pistol from my accessories box. **(D)**

Colors used include Black (No. 70.950) for the handkerchief, Earth Brown (No. 71.290) for the pants, Ivory (No. 70.918) for the stockings, and Flat Brown (No. 70.984) for the hair. The shirt is White (No. 70.951) and the coat is Red Leather (No. 70.818). I also applied various highlights with pastel pencils.

**MODELING TIP:** Tinfoil's flexibility makes it easy to work with, although it can break, so be careful. The scarf here was simple to make from foil, which also is useful for shaping capes, jackets, tents, pieces of cloth blown by the wind, flags, and sails for miniature boats.

D

**Figure 9**

This officer who grabs his hat because of the wind is hidden a bit behind the flag in the final diorama. It was difficult to place him as I needed to leave space for the last figures, taking into account the length of the flag and the space available in the boat.

Construction was simple, using a torso from the Barzso's American Minutemen kit and arms and legs from Historex (white plastic kits that include several figures from Napoleonic times with different postures). But I had to position the arms and legs to fit the scene, and space, before gluing them in place. **(A)**

Later I worked with Tamiya epoxy putty to extend the jacket, and shape the scarf, hair, and shirt sleeves that protrude somewhat from under the jacket. Other jacket details, such as the end of the sleeves, the lapels, and the belt are cut from a small strip of fine tinfoil. The rifle was already attached to his left hand. I painted it Silver (No. 70.997) and Flat Brown (No. 70.984), with a black wash. **(B)**

I also worked on the plastic hat, that had to be hollowed out with a burin (commonly used by wood ship modelers) so that it would fit the figure's head. **(C)**

**This Continental Army soldier is painted Dark Blue (No. 70.925), Vermilion (No. 70.909), and Dark Sand (No. 70.847) for the pants. Buttons and hat ornaments are trimmed in Gold (No. 70.996).**

Nearing the boat's stern I used a Beneito Miniatures Continental Army soldier that was stationed on a mound, in a winter environment, particularly good because he was wrapped in a small blanket. All I needed to do was use putty to make the blanket look a little larger. **(A)**

The figure also is white metal, which I like because it's easy to manipulate, especially its limbs. Here, with a mini-drill I made a tiny hole in the soldier's right hand so he could hold a rifle, **(B)**

After enlarging the blanket I added a bit of left arm from a Historex set figure, then added tin for the sleeve and covered the joint with putty. The legs belong to a soldier from Italeri's Napoleonic Wars French Supply Wagon (No. 6886) set. **(C)**

Colors for this figure include Ivory (No. 70. 918) for the blanket (including two decorative stripes in blue and gray), Khaki (No. 70.988) for pants, and Black (No. 70. 950) for shoes.

The rifle consists of Flat Brown (No. 70.984), Gunmetal Gray (No. 70.863), and Silver (No. 70. 997) accents. I applied a black wash to several areas and finished by airbrushing a diluted mixture of water, black paint, and matte varnish.

The hat, painted Light Gray (No. 70.990) and shaded with a black wash, was finished with dry-brushing of a light gray pigment. The hat is an accessory by Andrea Miniatures. Finally, I added highlights with an ivory pastel pencil.

Figure 10

A

B

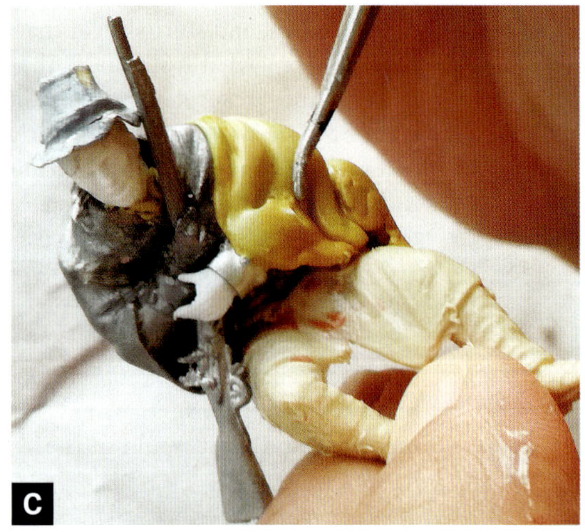

C

Again, this figure is a bit hard to see, but is one of the tense soldiers waiting to fight, yet not rowing. This young man has a taciturn look that I reproduced in as much detail as possible. But there was a lot of body work to get the arms and legs to fit. I used arms, hands, legs and torso from four figures before adding a hat from an Andrea Miniatures set. **(A)**

A remarkable amount of putty had to patiently be added to properly mimic the folds of the figure's thick winter coat and hood after attaching and sculpting the joins of the legs. After the putty was dry for the coat I worked on shaping the hood and adding a fur texture. **(B, C)**

Color was simple with Cork Brown (No. 70.843) for the coat and Gray-Green (No. 70.866) for pants and shirt underneath, a Light Green (No. 70.833) for leggings, and Black (No. 70.950) for footwear. The black hat also features a blue and red feather. which I imitated with a small piece of cotton. **(D, E)**

Figure 11

A

B

D

This figure had some peculiarities: the pose of the right hand on the weapon, and a kind of white bandage or bandana around the head. I also had to rebuild the weapon from my spares box because it had been broken. I fixed it with tinfoil.

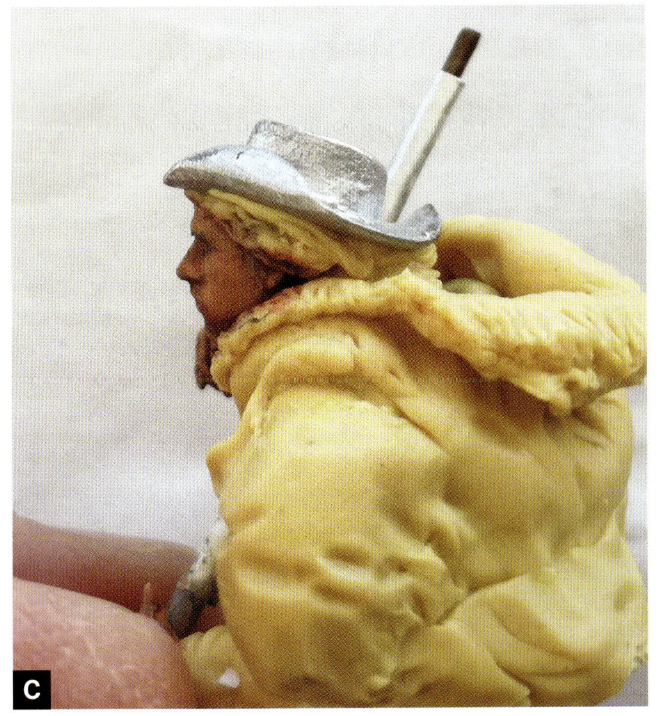
C

E

Figure 12

A

The final figure in the stern was among the most difficult due to its posture and repositioning its legs, arms and hands using parts from various figures. It is a somewhat forced pose as the rower seems hardly able to keep his balance while rowing, but maintaining it while adapting to the boat's movements. **(A)**

Again I worked carefully with Tamiya epoxy putty to sculpt the figure's thick hooded coat and Indian-style pants. **(B)** Next is the bag, which is made of tinfoil, and the fringes carefully cut and painted. **(C, D)**

Basically the paint here is more Cork Brown (No. 70.843) for the pants and Park Green Flat (No. 70.969) for the coat. For the hat I used Earth Brown (No. 71.290) and Ochre (No. 70.856), the highlights applied with a dry brush.

I created shadows and highlights by first applying a layer of retardant liquid and mixing the green with White (No. 70.951) and Black (No. 70. 950). Finally, I added highlights with a lemon green pastel pencil.

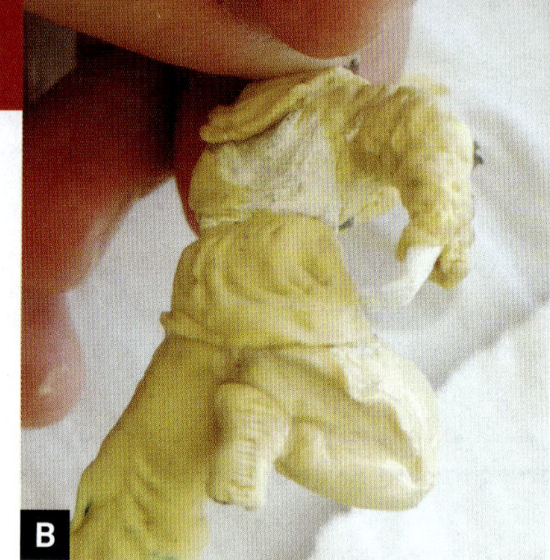

B

C

D

## THE DIORAMA

The structure and design of the diorama had some complexity, but always within a simple scenic concept. I tried to emulate the winter scene from Leutze's painting, the Delaware River full of blocks of ice, while the boat commanded by Washington tried to make its way to the shore. On the sides we see the banks of the river with abundant snow, some scattered plants, and a lot of ice.

# 6 STEPS FOR CREATING THE BASE

First I selected a wooden board as a base to draw where the river would flow before cutting white foam insulation to form the river banks, then adding layers of Das Pronto putty. Detailing here isn't necessary as much of this will be covered with snow eventually.

Next, I turned to painting the land and river bed, using Chocolate Brown (No. 70.872) for the earth and Dark Green (No. 70.970) and Dark Blue (No. 70.930) for the river bed. For shallower areas I mixed fresh paint to fade the tones, adding Light Green (No. 70.942).

To create artificial snow I used Green Stuff World's fake snow product. It is a fine snow that gives good results. I stuck it to the base using diluted white glue applied with a thick brush.

Once finished with this portion of the base, I placed transparent hard acetate barriers on the edges of the board to allow me to pour resin over the river portion to imitate its icy water. **(25)**

To ensure the watertightness of the diorama I attached the acetate with hot liquid silicone (using a glue gun usually sold in craft stores). The resin is that used in other dioramas in this book and made by La Pajarita (Varnish Finish Glass). **(26, 27)**

The liquid is poured out little by little once it has been mixed with the catalyst to accelerate its drying. I used several layers and it takes about 24 hours to dry.

Next came the most interesting challenge of the diorama: imitating the ice and floating ice blocks on the Delaware River.

After doing countless tests with different materials, transparent plastic, silicone, epoxy glues, etc. I came to a simple conclusion, the only way to imitate ice on that scale was to find a material that was malleable, whose hue was between white with some blue, and with a translucent texture. The solution was crushed peppermint candy white glued to a piece of transparent silicone.

I created the small blocks by crushing the peppermint with pliers and gluing them to transparent silicone bases (shoe insoles). The candies were a mix between Halls and other eucalyptus-scented candies. **(28, 29)**

Finally, I applied Vallejo transparent Dense Gel (No. 28.535) and transparent varnish to the entire water section to imitate movement.

I also added a few chunks of coarse salt to mimic the smaller ice chips, especially those near the main boat. A bit of touch-up around the scene included adding small pebbles and both coarse and fine salt crystals along with baking soda, to imitate smaller pieces of ice at the shoreline. **(30)**

25

26

27

28

29

30

## CHAPTER FIVE

**SKILLS**

Design and assemble a castle, with minimal background information

Combine three scales to obtain realistic photo effects

Create the effect of a burned wagon

**SCALES**

Cavalier: 1/32
Soldier: 1/35
Remaining figures: 1/72

# Siege of Rheinberg (1586-1590)

**This diorama** was inspired by an old engraving made by the Dutch artist Frans Hogenberg at the end of the 16th century. It shows a military operation featuring the Spanish Army (Tercios) on the outskirts of Rheinberg (now in Germany) during the Flanders Wars (1568-1648).

## The History

This scene takes place in the strategic enclave of Rheinberg, one of the main crossing points of the Rhine River between Cologne and the Dutch border. It represents the time period between Aug. 13, 1586 and Feb. 3, 1590, during the Eighty Years War, the War of Cologne, and Anglo-Spanish War (1585-1604).

After an initial siege in 1586, and a long blockade by Spanish forces until September 1589, Don Alessandro Farnese, commander of the Spanish army, sent a substantial force, with Peter Ernst, Count of Mansfeld, to lay siege to Rheinberg. Despite efforts by Maarten Schenk von Nydegger (until his death in the Assault on Nijmegen on Aug. 10, 1589), and Sir Francis Vere (1590), to free the fortress city, the Protestant garrison finally surrendered to the Spanish on Feb. 3, 1590. That didn't settle things. On Aug. 19, 1597, the Dutch army led by Mauricio de Nassau captured Rheinberg, but the following year the Spanish army of Flanders led by Don Francisco de Mendoza retook the strategic city, forcing the garrison to surrender. Rheinberg fell into Dutch hands again in successive counterattacks until the relentless incursion of the Spanish General Ambrosio Spínola during the 1605-1606 campaign.

**Here we see partial views of the diorama, showing the various scales used. First there is a 1/35 scale soldier pulling a donkey carrying war supplies (1); second is a 1/32 scale officer on horseback) with the soldier and his donkey in the background (2); and finally a 1/72 scale detail atop a small defensive castle with artillery pieces and their operators. (3)**

The diorama depicts the movement of warring Spanish troops commanded by Gen. Spínola next to two artillery pieces at a river site where Spanish soldiers were entrenched during those itinerant wars in which Rheinberg was continuously besieged as it changed hands. In these incursions, the small forts built to support ground troops became vitally important. They were equipped with thick walls, two or three batteries, access to the upper portions, in addition to a booth perhaps for protection and/or to supply ammunition. This diorama shows a small detachment momentarily retreating, but in an orderly manner.

**Creating a Visual Illusion:** Here you can see how scales work to create depth of field, the scales descending in size. The arc at the front of the diorama also shows that there are at least five photo points that will create realistic depth of field and therefore believable photos. To properly photograph the scene I added a printed photographic background to re-create an intensely cloudy sky. I captured the picture by closing the aperture to F22, commonly the smallest opening used in bright light conditions. That creates greater depth of field. I used a Nikon D3300 with an 18-55mm lens.

## THE DIORAMA'S GOAL

The object here was to translate the action of Franz Hogenberg's engraving into a diorama by focusing on select details from the drawing while bringing it to life with figures, including horses. Yet I also wanted to add details, such as the riverbank, a boat,wagon, and other elements, to add interest while mixing three scales.

Here we see the scale differentiation looking back from zone 2 to 1 with the 1/35 scale soldier pulling his donkey, and the 1/32 scale officer on horseback in back. Overall there are three zones, as seen in Image 4 (previous page), the final being 1/72 scale with the castle, boat, tree, two tents, and two horses. There also are the figures in the castle. Overall there are 11 figures in the scene.

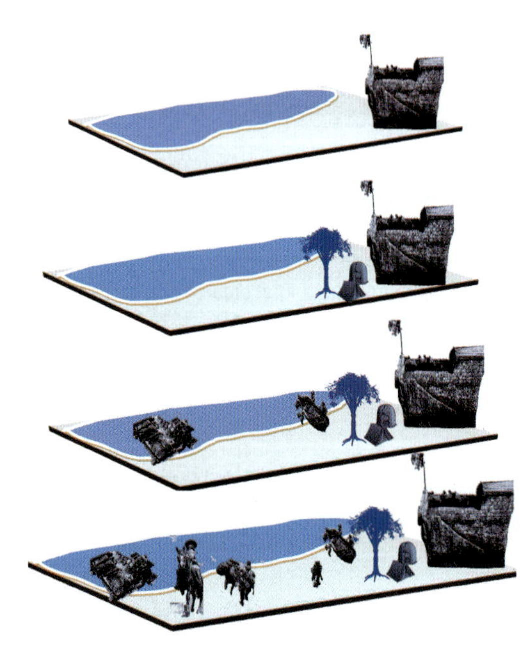

## 4 steps to placing elements in the diorama:

**Step 1:** First prepare the riverbed, painting the land with earthy and ochre tones, then place the already finished fortification.

**Step 2:** Place the tents and tree while finishing the ground.

**Step 3:** Add the water and elements in contact with the river, then place the boat and burned wagon.

**Step 4:** Finally place the figures to create the illusion of depth of field.

5

6

7

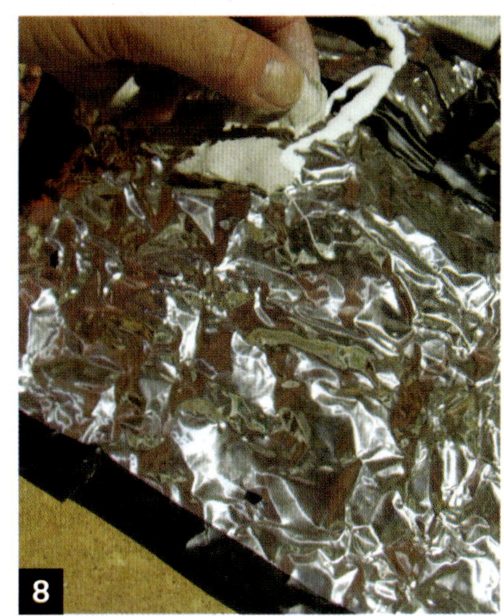

8

9

10

11

## Starting the build

Now that you have the background and some perspective on how the diorama will be arranged to feature the three scales, I'll describe the build in five phases, starting with the base and wrapping up with the final stage, broken into three parts, dealing with the figures.

### Phase 1: The base

Start with a light plywood board for a base, or use a bulletin board, one with a frame and smooth cork on one side. **(5)** Eager to learn a new skill I experimented with sheets of tinfoil, due to its ductility, to increase the land's surface area. I then added pieces of white foam insulation and added one plastic container that would be used in the next step. **(6-8)** I fixed the foil to the base with adhesive tape and found it was easy to add texture to the surface.

Once the land's varying slopes were glued in place I was careful to keep the formations in scale with the varying figures I would be adding so as not to overpower any of them, especially the smaller scale figures. For example I marked a river bank to be narrower by the area adjoining the 1/72 scale figures.

Next, I mixed Aguaplast powder with water and patiently covered the entire diorama's surface with the mix, avoiding excessive bubbles and clumps.

On the earthy area I applied a generous layer of Vallejo Gray Sand gel (No. 26.215) mixed with Earth Texture Brown Earth (No. 26.219) gel. **(9, 10)** This creates an excellent finish, and its hardness is especially forgiving when mixed with other acrylics. **(11)**

Once dry, I airbrushed with a variety of Vallejo paints, which I use throughout the build, except as noted. Here I mixed Ochre Brown (No. 70.856), Yellow Brown (No. 71.246) and Chocolate Brown (No. 70.872) tones, using Dark Sand (No. 70.847), Matte Black (No. 70.950), and Earth Texture Brown Earth gel, trying to create a lighter tone closest to the river. **(12)** I also applied washes using Brown Glaze (No. 70.854) and Medium Green (No. 70.891) before adding fragments of dry moss and pebbles to create, without going overboard, the presence of a river bank. **(13)**

12

13

14

16

Model railroading accessories often help achieve realistic effects in dioramas. Here I have used textured plastic roofing material found at a hobby store.

15

17

The castle's storage room for ammunition was made with clay bricks, so I used bricks from a hobby kit along with balsa wood slats to frame the area.

## Phase 2: The castle

I used that overturned plastic container on the base as the foundation of the small castle that covers the flank of the river at the diorama's far end. I knew that it would need to be surrounded by the building materials of the day, which meant imitating the stonework of the area, along with sand, mortar, and the usual clay materials in the site's wetlands. **(14)** My research of the artist's engraving had verified the presence of streams and muddy grounds near the castle.

So I applied Das Pronto and Aguaplast putty to the plastic container to mimic the stone texture's base, But I admit to difficulties as the container's flexible nature did not easily allow the putties to adhere, leading to cracks. **(15)**

So at the top I created thick balsa wood walls to frame the container while also building balsa stairs and adding scale bricks from a model railroad construction kit. This resulted in a realistic castle exterior, especially after painting. **(16-20)**

I started the painting process with Medium Gray Primer (No. 70.987),

18

Again I turned to balsa wood to build the staircase, and hobby bricks to make the steps.

19

The Aguaplast layer must be very thin and applied to the entire castle, including the stairs, to seal the structure. The advantage of working with this thin paste is that it dries hard and is easy to work with later using a hobby knife or scribing tool, and the surface readily accepts paint.

20

Once the Aguaplast layer has dried, it was simple to imitate the stone's texture by marking it with a hobby knife to create silhouettes of the castle stones.

21

22

followed by a coat of Tamiya Buff (XF-57), **(21)**

Next I highlighted the jagged stones with a variety of colors, such as browns and greens to imitate moisture. **(22)** As the paint was drying I airbrushed a diluted solution of matte acrylic black to create shadows, something I used at various points of the diorama. Washes using Black Glaze (No. 70.855) as a base are especially useful for pulling out the detail and texture in castle stones and other stonework. **(23, 24)**

23

24

Using a wash of diluted Black Glaze is vital to aging the stones and painting with greens and browns to show the impact of humidity, deterioration and smoke, on both the side walls and castle's floor up top where the cannon are located. Dry-brushing with those colors and using pastel pencils added the final highlights to the stones.

The finished castle looks realistic and adapts to the conditions of the terrain that we want to present around it, including the horse, which again adds scale.

## Phase 3: A burned wagon, a tree, and tents

The wagon initially was assembled for a project I abandoned. It was painted with Flat Brown (No. 70.984) and darkened with Brown Glaze. **(26)**

But for this scene I decided to place it in the foreground and make it appear as if it had burned. So I broke it rather indelicately with pliers. The scorched wood look was simple to create with black and gray washes and then a pastel white pencil used in the corners. I also added a rusty chain and used a black pastel pencil on the most heavily burned areas. **(27)**

I added a damaged carriage to the scene, thinking that in any diorama set in the 16th century there are certainly no tanks, but wagons and carriages were prevalent to move military gear. Putting the wagon in the foreground gives it a certain prominence.

Next I made a tree, first locating a branch from a nearby forest. It fit the scale, 1/72. Then I added a few twigs with superglue. I liked these as they were covered in lichens, which although dried gave a convincing green tint to my tree. **(28)**

Spraying the tree's entire crown with hairspray made the branches sticky enough for me to then sprinkle on artificial grass of varying shades of green. The result brought some color to the scene. **(29)**

Tree complete I moved on to scratchbuilding the tents. I made wire frames (painted black) and then covered them with paper dipped in a mixture of water and white glue. **(30)** I again used Hofenberg's engraving to inspire the tents' shapes, but didn't add much detail. I painted them German Gray (No. 70.995), then brushed on dry pastels to add weathering.

When the completed tree is in place its realism is easily seen, thanks to adding artificial grass and dry-brushing yellow to add depth.

**The original boat was white metal. I only added a few balsa wood planks before painting and weathering.**

## Phase 4: The boat and river

This detail of a small boat with soldiers trying to pull it ashore centers attention on one of the most striking corners of the diorama because the dynamic posture of these men contrasts with the apparent slowness of the rider in the foreground. **(31)**

The 1/72 boat kit, a felucca, marketed by the Italian firm Amati, was ideal for this scene, but needed quite a few improvements to look realistic. Among other things, it required suitable finishing to imitate worn wood, which I accomplished with Citadel's smoke-colored ink. **(32, 34)**

For weaponry I cut several swords from a set of Revell figures and attached them to the bottom of the felucca. I found the boxes in the Airfix Forward Command Post set (04380-5), and the fruit baskets came from an accessory set that Preiser distributes for use with model railroads.

To make the water, I worked with polyester resin. To create more cloudiness in the artificial water (working from artificial resin) I poured in a few drops of Flat Brown paint. **(35, 36)**

Once the resin was dry, I applied several layers of Heavy Gel Gloss (No. 27.592) to sculpt movement into the river's waters. **(37, 38)**

## Phase 5: The figures

I searched for information about the Flanders wars from different sources, taking data from the Spanish magazine *Desperta Ferro*. There I saw a figure with clothing similar to the one I modeled as the soldier guiding the pack donkey. For the rest of the figures I was inspired by the paintings of Augusto Ferrer-Dalmau, especially one titled *El Camino Español*. This was an incredible reference for details about the clothing of the Spanish infantry and cavalry in Flanders during the 16th and 17th century.

To design and assemble the figures in the three scales I combined sections and fragments from figures as follows:

**Many details can be extracted from great artworks such as those of the Flanders Wars by Spanish painter Augusto Ferrer-Dalmau. Here we see the artist painting *Rocroi, el último Tercio* (2011).** *Image: Augusto Ferrer-Dalmau, Wikimedia Commons*

**1. Cavalier (1/32 scale)**
This is the Airfix figure Cavalier/Roundhead (No. 02558-0), a beautiful 54mm figure on horseback. It's a 1979 kit, but still can be found on eBay. I only made three modifications to the figure, the shirt whose side openings I made with pieces of paper; the crossed belts on the cuirass (breast and back plate), made with tinfoil; and the wide belt, made with ribbon tied laterally to his waist with a thick knot made of white Milliput putty. **(39, 40)**

My paint scheme included White (No. 70.951) for the shirt with wide collars; Black (No. 70.950) for the hat, hair and beard; Buff (No. 70.976) for the bodice and skirt; and Silver (No. 70.997) for all metal parts. I darkened those areas with Black Glaze. Meanwhile the hat's feather and waist cloth were painted Scarlet Red (No. 70.817) while the belts, gloves, and boots were painted two shades of brown, U.S. Field Drab (No. 70.873) and Chocolate Brown. The horse also is painted Chocolate Brown with highlights of Medium Brown (No. 70.860) **(41, 42)**

41

39

40

42

**The original Airfix figure was well detailed, but I had to use great care to adapt it to a period Spanish uniform. My tools were putty, tinfoil, and wet paper mixed with white glue. The horse was painted following the Airfix instructions, using various dark browns and a black wash, then a dry-brushing of cinnamon tones to add accents. I improved the straps by making them with tin tape cut to fit.**

**2. Soldier and donkey (1/35 scale)**
This duo, a Spanish Tertio soldier and his donkey, during a break in the battles, is one of my favorite compositions. I worked intensively on the wounded figure from the Master

Box set, Road to the Rear (No. 3558) to transform the uniform of a German WWII soldier into the uniform of a Spanish soldier from the 16th-17th century. I had to remove pockets to add details such as the belt and then deliberately lengthen the coat, again with putty. **(43)**

The donkey is from Tamiya's Livestock Set (No. 35128), but has been laden with leftover accessories and equipment from my parts box in an attempt to make him look like the pack animal he is. **(44)**

Colors for the soldier are similar to the cavalier and include an Ice Yellow (No. 70.858) coat; a White shirt, Earth Brown pants; and Black boots, hair and beard. His hat is painted U.S. Field Drab and I finished the lighter areas with pastel-colored pencils. I didn't want to use the dry-brush technique as that can easily mar the finish of a larger scale figure where stroke marks can become more evident. **(45)**

43

44

45

**To make the donkey feel more like a pack animal I loaded it with various supplies, such as a bag to carry personal items (a leftover from a Spanish soldier figure of the same period). I also added a sack, a Spanish pikeman's helmet, a rope, a wood barrel, and blanket.**

## The small figures (1/72 scale)

The nine 1/72 scale figures are taken from Revell's Thirty Years War Imperial Artillery set (No. 02566) and had to be placed in three different scenarios. There are artillerymen in the castle, several pulling a boat out of the river, and one isolated rider with a horse tied to the castle's base.

I tried to incorporate additional details to enhance the realism of this scene's more distant troops. Especially concerned with the ability to take realistic photos, I added cannon balls near the cannons, other weapons, and then a few supplies in the boat, along with a few random elements.

To help unify the scene I decided to retain a similar aesthetic as the remainder of the diorama when it came to painting these 1/72 scale figures.

In reality there were no compulsory uniforms at the time. That didn't happen, mostly, until the 18th century. So I took some liberties when painting these small figures. But I drew inspiration from the color scheme of the officer on horseback, especially emphasizing the Buff colored jacket, Earth Brown pants and Black hat.

All of the figures were treated with shadow washes, using both Black and Brown Glazes to show wear.

Finally, the pants of the gunners in the castle were all painted Dark Blue (No. 70.930). **(46-48)**

46

47

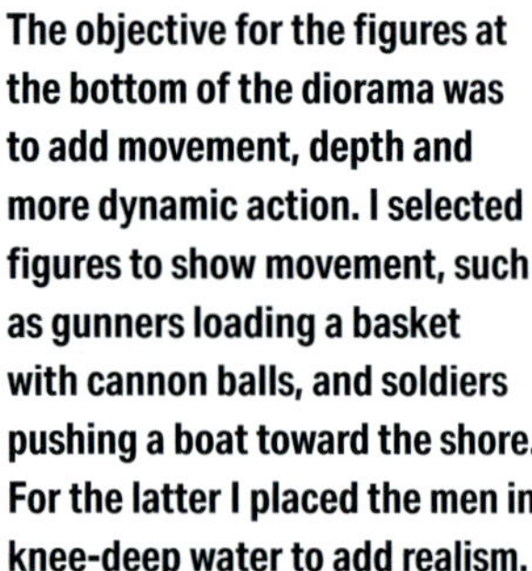

**The objective for the figures at the bottom of the diorama was to add movement, depth and more dynamic action. I selected figures to show movement, such as gunners loading a basket with cannon balls, and soldiers pushing a boat toward the shore. For the latter I placed the men in knee-deep water to add realism.**

48

## CHAPTER SIX

# Pedro Menéndez de Avilés sails to Florida

**SKILLS**

Find the optimal position of two different scale objects to create the most realistic photographic angle.

Paint the ocean different shades of blue to achieve realistic results.

Find an ideal way to hide the electrical system under the ocean waves.

**SCALES**

Ship: 1/600
Figures: 1/35

**Pedro Menéndez de Avilés** (1519-1574) is an inspirational figure. He was Adelantado of Florida, Admiral and General of the Spanish Army of the Indies and, in the summer of 1565, **Menéndez** was beginning the journey that would lead him to retake Florida for Spain. He would take Fort Caroline and other settlements of the French Huguenots while also founding St. Augustine, Fla. That's the oldest city in the United States, celebrating its 450th anniversary in 2015. A handmade 1/30 scale replica of his ship was given by the city of Avilés, the Spanish conqueror's hometown, to St. Augustine to mark the anniversary.

I wasn't so lucky to have such a galleon on hand to create this diorama marking Menéndez landing in Florida. He had captained the galleon *San Pelayo*, but there are no 1/600 scale kits of that ship. So I used a Heller kit, which is slightly different from the original galleon (four masts instead of three, more guns, etc.). But the Heller kit is proportionally similar to the Menéndez ship.

The idea of combining two scales on a small base, which consisted of a small boat approaching a large sailing ship, had been in my head for some time. Here's how I brought it together.

**The world-famous explorer Pedro Menéndez de Avilés is immortalized here dressed in the classic loose, black, velvety coat with the Cross of the Order of Santiago emblazoned on the chest, and a high-collared shirt.** *Image: Francisco de Paula Martí /Library of Congress*

## Phase I: The boat

The boat needed to be designed from scratch to accommodate the small crew. I chose 1/35 scale for the versatility of positioning it, and because there are many 1/35 plastic figures to chose from. I find them much more manageable than white metal figures for altering their sitting positions. I also wanted to photograph the scene with a sunset background, so thought small lights on the boat and ship would enhance the scene's realism.

The artistic photo angle chosen required the rowing sailor to be in the boat's stern with the captain facing forward and near the boat's bow. Meanwhile the galleon should be at anchor in the distance with its transom toward the camera.

The boat started as one piece of wood sold as an accessory for wooden boats. It has been several years since I made it, so I've forgotten the brand. But it came in a plastic bag.

I made marks and then created holes with a punch to add tack to the sides, giving the small boat a little more height. To weather it I used black shoe polish paste (not liquid), followed with a wash of Vallejo Black Glaze (No. 70.855). I use that to create a patina and use Vallejo products here unless otherwise noted.

**Once the boat was finished, but before placing the crew, I thought about the accessories that should be stowed in it. I gathered and finished them to add life to the vessel.**

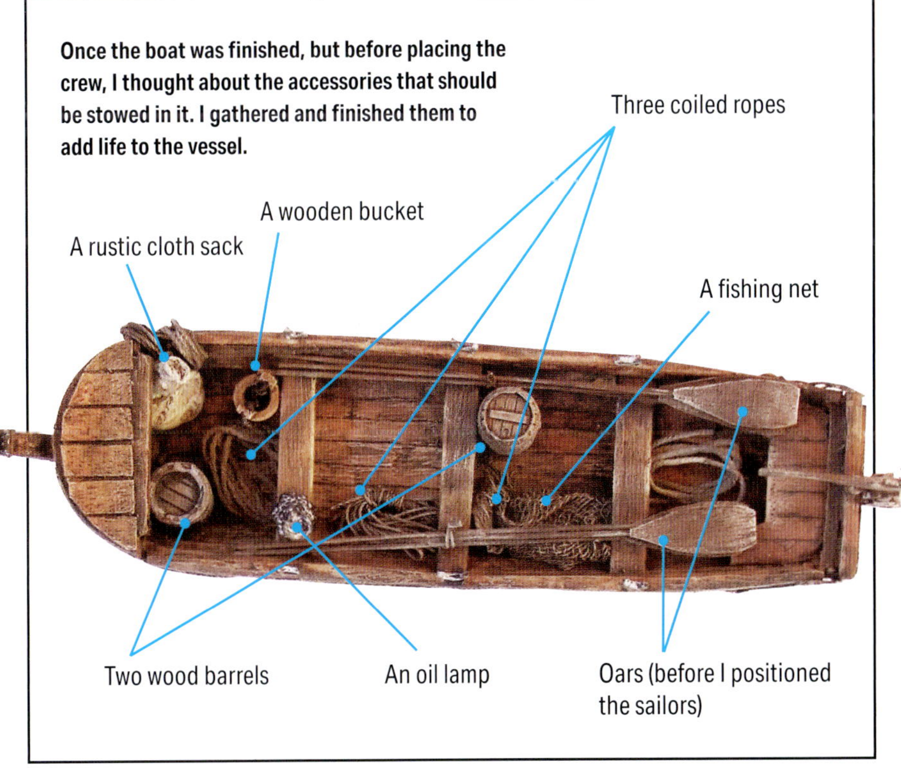

## Phase II: The figures, and a lamp

With the boat complete I turned my attention to the figures while also planning to put a small bulb on the boat in an effort to imitate an oil lamp next to the captain. First I used a mini-drill to create a small hole adjacent to where the Spanish captain would be seated.

The lamp was fashioned from a piece of jewelry and clear plastic tubing to portray the lamp, then painted its edges Black (No. 70.950) to help it blend with the boat and the captain. **(1)**

I made the captain by bonding parts (torso, arms, legs, hands) of various 1/35 scale Tamiya figures that I had in my spares box. I tried to adapt the figure to the natural posture of a man sitting on a boat's bench seat, then worked on his attire. **(2)**

To imitate the boots and doublet I used Milliput Superfine White putty, while the ruff was a challenge. But I found a plastic tablecloth with fine white plastic frets that mimics embroidery. I cut a tiny semicircle and glued it to his neck, then added a tiny metal chain I had found at a jewelry store for a convincing look. **(3-10)**

Next I made his belt from a piece of tinfoil, which was simple. However, creating the captain's hat and coat took more finesse.

**I fabricated the captain's hat from a small bucket, a basket found in a Preiser accessory set (No. 17502), and a rounded piece of tinfoil. Then I painted it with Flat Earth (No. 70.983).**

**To make the coat, I first cut a piece of black construction paper to the appropriate size and shape before soaking it in a 50/50 mix of water and white glue.**

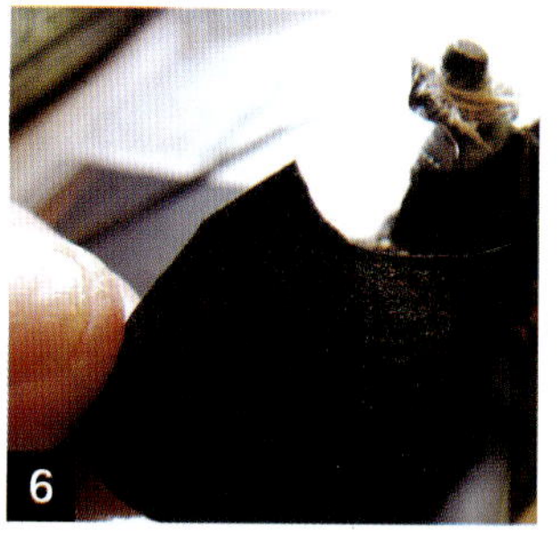

**Once soaked, the paper is wrapped around the captain figure and allowed to conform to his back for a perfect fit once it dries.**

**To decorate his chest with the Cross of the Order of Santiago, I found a copy on the internet, then printed it to the proper size before cutting and pasting it to the captain, again soaking the paper in the water and white glue mixture.**

**10 Next I fabricated the captain's sword from a piece of spare plastic from other models, a piece of jewelry, and a pin.**

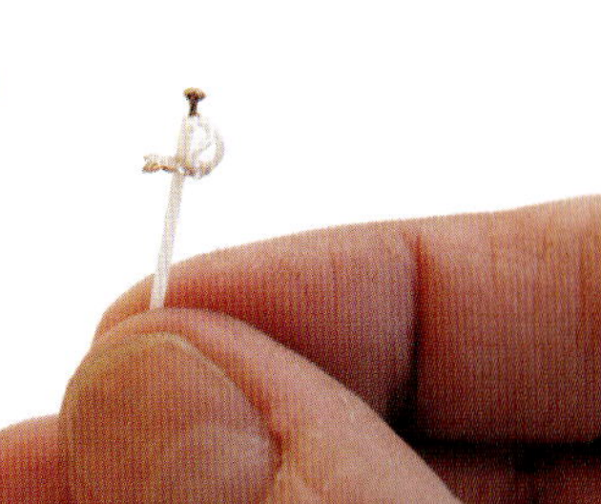

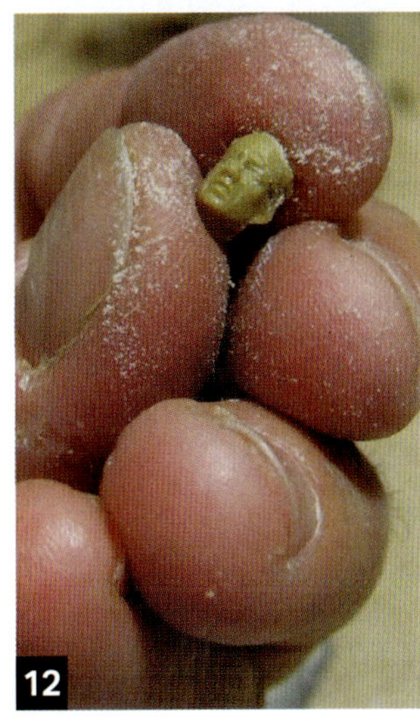

**Realism often depends on how well you paint the eyes. I used Ivory (No. 70.918) and White (No. 70.951) paint before marking the pupil with a black dot and adding a fine line on the upper eyelid.**

Creating the boat's oarsman is next. Again I combined different figure's body parts to get what I needed for the scene. These were from the Master Box 1/35 set, Road to the Rear (No. MB3558) featuring five WWII German soldiers accompanying a wagon carrying a wounded soldier. Several of the figures' sitting positions were attractive enough to give me good alternatives. I chose one with a slightly hunched torso, legs in a sitting position, arms and hands properly gripping what would be oars.

Next, I filed the head and created hair with Milliput putty. Finally a little more putty work to create the proper wrap of clothing and boots completed the figure before painting.

I used White for the shirt, Cork Brown (No. 70.843 for the coat, Cavalry Brown (No. 70.982) for the trousers, and Black for the hat and boots. Once the figure was dry I applied a thin layer of diluted Black Glaze. **(11-15)**

## Phase III: The galleon

Pyro was the only brand with a small-dimension Spanish galleon kit (approximately 1/600 scale) of the period 1530 to 1550. Revell had a 1/450 scale kit, but the Pyro has more details such as guns, planks, and poles, making it better for diorama purposes. The Pyro ship also was ideal for the 18-inch square wood base I was using, and would look convincing with minimal work on the deck's texture and detailing its cannons and sails.

Assembly was quickly completed due to the minimal number of parts. **(16, 17)** Plus the cannons were already modeled on the deck. I added some homegrown details, such as a gravure that mimics a railing and comes from a model railroading set sold for house dioramas. Once I mounted the masts I painted the entire ship with Flat Earth, followed by a wash of Black Glaze. **(18-20)**

16

17

**Creating a strong bond is key with the ship's hull, so I used superglue and then wrapped thick rubber bands around the hull to keep the joins tightly sealed.**

18

19

**I applied a thin layer of Tamiya Putty dissolved in pure acetone to cover mounting slots and imperfections around the ship's deck.**

20

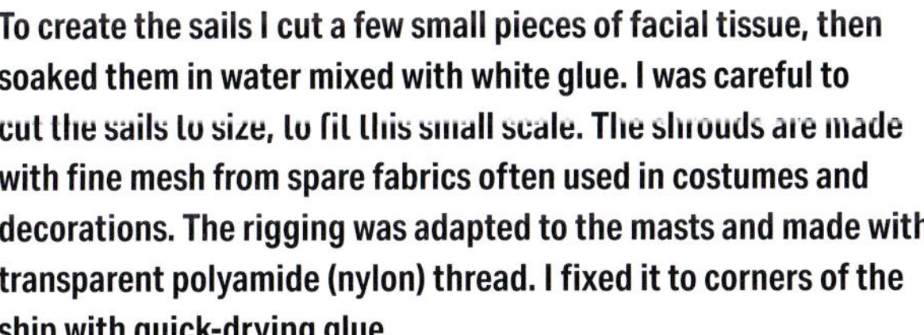

To create the sails I cut a few small pieces of facial tissue, then soaked them in water mixed with white glue. I was careful to cut the sails to size, to fit this small scale. The shrouds are made with fine mesh from spare fabrics often used in costumes and decorations. The rigging was adapted to the masts and made with transparent polyamide (nylon) thread. I fixed it to corners of the ship with quick-drying glue.

## When Spanish galleons linked Europe to America

From the mid-16th century until the 18th, Spain dominated a wide range of Atlantic and Pacific routes. The galleon (first as a defensive, then offensive vessel), played a crucial role. Its structure changed with the addition of ships of the line to conventional naval fleets.

Along with the inherent dangers of bad weather (hurricanes and severe storms), and the harsh conditions of life aboard, the main enemy was buccaneers and privateers, especially the British. They were called sea dogs who forcefully aggravated the great Spanish fleet, intercepting it and making off with the ships' valuable cargo. This led shipbuilders to construct tall ships of considerable size to repel the pirates, emphasizing the ships artillery and munitions. Later these cannon touted four wheels to make them both more maneuverable and easier to load or unload.

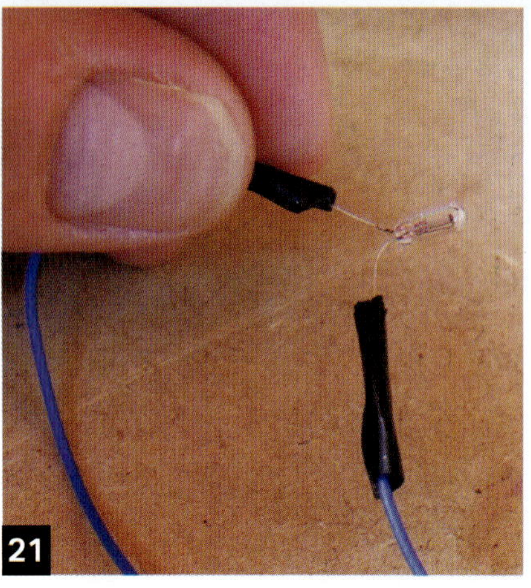

**It's important to calculate the length of the wire that will supply power to the small bulb in the stern so that it can be connected to a power source beyond the diorama.**

Before finally fitting the galleon into the diorama, I made a hole in the hull, under the waterline, to place a flexible tube that could house a wire for a small bulb that would take its place at the stern, where I would place another lantern. I also made a hole in the bridge of the awning, near the stern, to house the bulb and its corresponding wires. It is important to carefully connect the wires securely before inserting the bulb into the tube so that the connections do not come loose. **(21-24)**

## Phase IV: The sea and electrical system

The sea needed careful planning. As in the diorama of the Roman senator, detailed in Chapter 8, I liked the idea of contrasting a larger wave in the foreground by the 1/35 scale boat, and a smaller wave near the galleon. The wave volumes were created with strips of white insulating foam cut into small pieces. I would attach and finish these once I had their locations set. **(25, 26)**

But I also had to account for the electrical system's location. In a small diorama, the electrical system must be well controlled. I bought an adapter to convert 220 volts into 12 volts, the voltage normally required for micro-bulbs commonly used in model railroad layouts, and what I'd chosen for this project. **(27)**

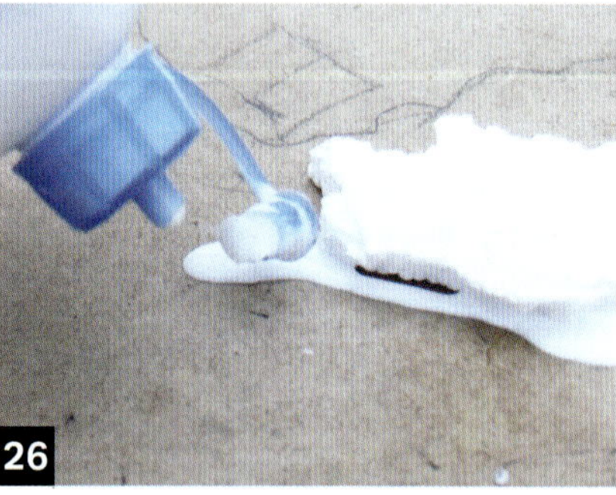


**While designing the base, I placed pieces of white insulating foam in various spots to simulate what the final composition would look like and how I could adjust it to make a compelling photograph.**

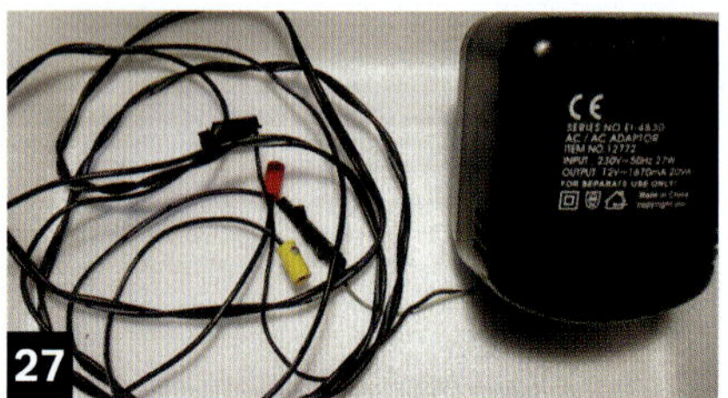

## Key positioning

It's important to test place the galleon and small boat in numerous locations before gluing anything in place. Having the galleon's stern with its lit lantern at an attractive angle was a key to the main photo I wanted. Looking at the scene from above, it's clear the best photo points will be in an arc behind the boat's stern. We also get a better understanding of how combining the scales works and see how the foam is used to create waves.

I also put the entire electrical system through a transparent plastic tube to protect the wires, both the one that starts from the boat and the one that comes out of the galleon. **(28, 29)** The flexible clear tube, about one centimeter in diameter, is helpful in safely isolating the diorama's electrical system to keep it from being damaged by putty and paste.

To show wave movement and to form the usual relief of the sea waves, I used Das Pronto fresh putty with the help of various sculpting tools. **(30)** When the entire surface had completely dried, I covered it with a layer of Aguaplast. **(31, 32)** Then I placed the galleon and the boat in their correct positions, to visualize what I was sure would be an interesting angle for the primary photo highlighting the depth of field created by the two scales.

28

29

30

31

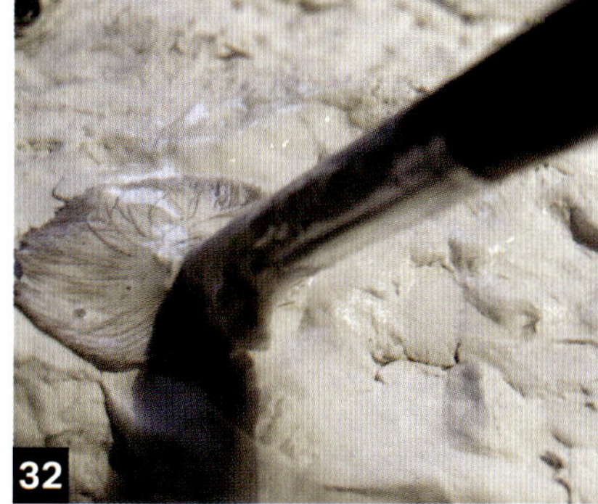

32

I was nearing the finish line now, so I turned my attention to painting the waves several shades of blue to give them depth. I used Ultramarine Blue (No. 72.022), Oxford Blue (No. 70.807) and Royal Blue (No. 70.809).

Before the acrylics dried I mixed in lighter shades with the darker paint to create lighter highlights atop the waves' crests, then added foam by using a mixture of white paint and Water Effects Foam & Snow (No. 26.231). **(33- 36)** Later, I applied greasy strokes with Manley school blue wax crayons of different shades for further highlights. **(37)**

33

34

35

36

37

**One of the last steps was making a small slit in the waves so that the boat's oar could realistically dip into the sea. That was enhanced by adding a few droplets of transparent silicone to create a real splash.**

## CHAPTER SEVEN

**SKILLS**

Creating a realistic water effect.

Painting and detailing small figures.

Creating and detailing a port environment.

**SCALES**

Main scene: 1/72
Tower: 1/87

# Trade with the Hanseatic League

**This diorama's design** started from a simple idea linked to a marine environment. I wanted to create an attractive backdrop for the 1/72 scale medieval boat model made by Zvezda. My thought was that the kit would fit nicely into a small dock in an urban setting. My choice was to dock the boat at a small North Sea port during the early 15th century. There it would be trading with the Hanseatic League, or Hansa, which was born as a federation of cities in northern Germany and included communities of German merchants in the Baltic Sea, the Netherlands, Norway, Sweden, England, Poland, part of Finland and Denmark, as well as regions that are now part of Estonia and Latvia.

## Phase I: The boat and its crew

I started by building the medieval boat produced by Zvezda, and placing a helmsman and merchant aboard. The model itself is simple to make, the key build consideration being to avoid excess glue.

Luckily Hecker & Goros makes a variety of medieval and Hanseatic figures, so I easily found a couple I could piece together to steer the boat, along with a merchant to stand in the bow while observing a couple that is waiting on shore for the boat to dock.

A bird's-eye view of the scene from the harbor shows the basic elements that have been used to imply movement, the sea, the boat, a man who is about to throw a rope to the boat, plus a wagon and horseman heading in opposite directions.

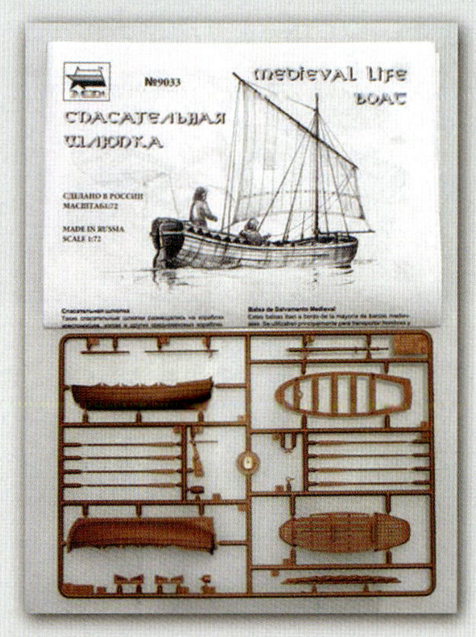


Zvezda's boat (No. 9033) offers an unblemished finish with an especially fine texture, in this case the wood planks, oars, and more.

**The merchant (1) is from Hecker & Goros, but to adapt the exact position of the sailor handling the boat's rudder I had to craft a figure by combining a torso, arms and legs from others. (2) I drew my parts from the following: Hansa crew (Hecker & Goros), Conquistadores (Caesar Miniatures), and a soldier from Italeri's Napoleonic Wars/French Supply Wagon kit, respectively.**

Having assembled the crew and boat I turned to painting the craft, starting with a Medium Brown (No. 71.038) for the entire vessel, again using Vallejo paints unless otherwise noted. Once dry I gave the boat a wash of diluted Black (No. 70.950) to age the craft and add depth to its finish. Next I dry-brushed Ivory (No. 70.918) along with subtle brushstrokes of varying shades of brown mixed with a paint retarder for acrylics to delay drying and facilitate tonal melding. For various highlights and shadows I created different washes using colors such as Black, Medium Brown, White (No. 70.951), Dessert Tan (No. 71.122), Yellow Ochre (No. 70.913), and Dark Red (No. 70.946). **(3)**

Next, I worked to further define the wood grain along with sail details using a Rotring pen. **(4)** I also added small strokes of light using pastel pencils of different colors. To complete

the boat's cargo I added accessories one might find in a boat, including ropes, barrels, and wine jugs from Italeri and Valdemar kits used elsewhere. **(5)**

I adapted the sail from a piece included in Imai´s Greek warship kit (1/250 scale) because the size looked adequate. **(6)** I also added a fishing net made of sterile gauze soaked in a 50/50 solution of water and white glue, then painted it with Tamiya Buff (XF-57).

## Phase II: The figures and wagon

To create the feeling of movement among the 10 figures throughout the diorama I had to analyze the poses available among figures already available commercially. The best way that I found was to consult the website, www.plasticsoldierreview.com.

That led me to buy and use a variety of figures from multiple kits, including, Napoleonic Wars French Supply Wagon (Italeri No. 6886S), Hanseatic Cogue Crew (Valdemar), Medieval Siege Troops (Orion, No. 72019), Spanish Conquistadores (Caesar Miniatures), Medieval Tournament (Italeri No. 6108), and Hansa Cogg captain and crew (Hecker & Goros).

Placing them would be a challenge, but my thought was that each had to have a function, while also showing movement. Each had to be doing something in the scene.

I began on the left, placing a citizen pouring water from a bucket into the sea, where I also inserted several floating items. While on the right a knight in armor rides the opposite direction of the detailed wagon. **(7, 8)**

Meanwhile, the driver of the wagon (carrying fresh fruit and vegetables) has stopped to talk with someone in front of the small shipyard. **(9)** On the dock, a wealthy couple waits for the arrival of the boat of Hanseatic merchants, who carry several wine barrels in their small boat. **(10)**

The wagon came from the Italeri Napoleonic Wars French Supply Wagon kit and there were not many modifications to be made, except for emphasizing the exterior wood's texture. I painted the whole wagon with Brown Earth gel (No. 26.219), and later applied a Dark Brown Wash (No. 76.514) heavily diluted with water. **(11)**

7

8

9

10

**Painting these small figures was simple. I used flat colors and washes created with black or dark brown to emphasize the folds and textures of a their clothes. Since the backgrounds and roadways were cream or gray, I thought it most dramatic to use various striking shades of red, blue, or purple, for much of their clothing.**

11

**In this finished shot you see how the painting and texture of the wooden wagon stands out and creates more realism in the scene.**

## Phase III: The base and sea

The base is wood with a thick layer of white foam insulation glued on top, while the steps down to the port's pier were made of wood. The pier's landing and wall were formed with Das Pronto clay. **(12, 13)** It was left to dry and the paving stones were worked individually with a hobby knife. Then the entire port's courtyard was coated with a thick layer of Aguaplast, a plasterlike material, to resemble a stone surface. **(14)**

Next I cut heavy acetate sheets to roughly the same dimensions as the diorama's foam base. I placed that under the foam, then sealed the edges with silicone to create a small pool where I would create the sea, without the liquid leaking out. **(15)** To create the sea I used a transparent liquid (two components) similar to the resin called Finish Glass, marketed by the Spanish brand, La Pajarita. Other resin brands are available at hobby stores or online. But I like this brand because it dries quickly and is not 100% transparent, which helps it look more uniform. **(16, 17)**

Just when it was about to set, I used a spatula to create a very light swell (quite complex since the resin always tends to return to its original position) and added foam details with transparent silicone and white paint working carefully with extremely fine brushes. I knew that the line between perfect and spoiled was thin, so took great care not to try this before the resin was nearly set.

It also was important that the seabed in front of the pier be as realistic as possible, so I added several moss fragments and simulated stones with cork fragments (bark of different trees used by gardeners or in Christmas scenes) and glued those to the sea bottom where it connects to the base of the pier. A layer of white glue was also spread with a brush that finally dried transparently over the entire sea bottom. **(16)**

12

13

14

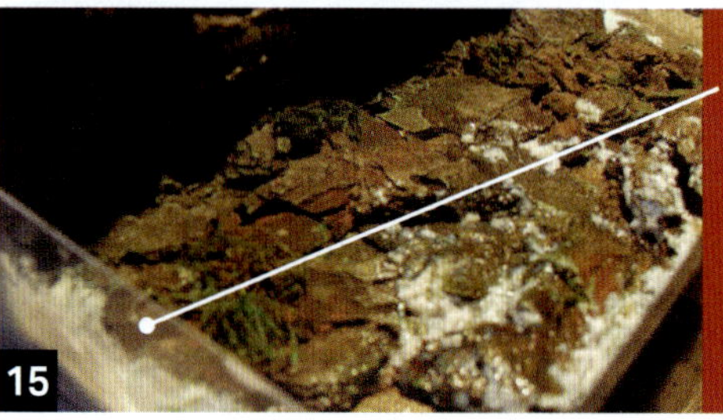

15

I cut sheets of transparent acetate to fit around the base of the diorama and meet the seawalls, then sealed them to the base and walls with silicone, making a waterproof pool in which I poured the resin that emulates the sea.

16

17

For realism I added a few floating elements to the water, including an old barrel, several pieces of wood, and remnants of a damaged ship.

18

19

## Phase IV: The port and shipyard

The port's front was handmade with small slats of hand-cut balsa wood and a Warhammer house whose door had to be reduced to slightly change the house's scale (marketed at 28mm). I then painted it with Ivory, Medium Brown, and Medium Gray (No. 70.870) then aged with an airbrushing of Black Glaze (No. 70.855) washes. The roof was outlined with various pastel pencils. **(18)**

The adjoining shipyard's exterior and interior wood panels all were treated with black and brown shoe polish paste, pastels, and a gentle dry-brushing of Dark Sand (No. 70.847).

To create more separation of the wood slats I marked them with a black ultra-fine permanent marker.

20

The boat is from Artesanía Latina to which I added details around its support beams, including real sawdust glued to the floor and boat, a barrel, and a ladder that connects the boathouse to the port building. There I added a carpenter climbing the ladder to add a bit of action to the scene. **(19, 20)**

Small details were needed to help set the scene. I added an old chain, a bollard, a barrel, and a fishing net. **(21, 22)** The cobblestones were painted separately, mixing Medium Gray with different shades of brown, yellow, green, and AK Interactive's Red Brick (No. 11093), treated with a diluted Black wash. Dry-brushing with Light Gray (No. 70.990) added highlights.

No detail is too small to add, and I remember my friend, Alex Curiá, a good modeler, told me the shipyard door was missing hinges. I stewed on it for awhile, then found a solution, small guns from a model ship. **(22)**

21

22

Here we see a lower position of the tower correctly placed. Note the fine detailing of the tiles and timbers, thanks to a careful job using a variety of pastel pencils.

## Phase V: The 1:87 scale tower

The idea of placing a slightly smaller scale tower in the background to add further depth came later when a model railroading friend gave me the tower. I fixed it up a bit, deciding it served as another example of using multiple scales in a diorama. **(23-25)** I had to make some fixes with superglue before adding a layer of Tamiya Putty to fix a few imperfections. Finally, I painted the tower with various Vallejo acrylics and finished detailing with a dry brush and pastel pencils. **(26)**

## CHAPTER EIGHT

**SKILLS**

Working with two-part epoxy putty.

Molding a dynamic sea surface.

Painting a realistic sea.

**SCALES**

Ship: 1/160
Figure: 1/20

# Pax Romana

**Following the conceptual approach** explained throughout this book of combining two or more scales in a diorama, I was inspired by an old book and drawing of a Roman port in peace times. The image included an anchored cargo ship within a port while in the foreground is the stern of another ship moving away from dock while a pensive man on board observes the undocking operation. He is a Roman senator of the 1st century, sailing on a cloudy evening.

The diorama's title is *Pax Romana* due to the scene's historical timeframe of between 27 BC and 180 AD. This is known as the Roman Empire's moment of maximum pacification and territorial and economic expansion. To enliven the dock I added figures to the original Pyro kit, whose scale is not specified, but is roughly 1/160. For inspiration I used this image I found in the 1995 Editorial Folio book *La Aventura del Mar: el Hombre y el Mar, De Homero al Titanic (The Adventure of the Sea: Man and the Sea).*

### Combining two scales

If we want to effectively combine two model scales it's best to test the different-sized objects to see if they will fit well within a photo frame. I started with the original Roman ship kit launched in the 1960s by Pyro and produced in about 1/160 scale. Finding a suitable large scale Roman figure (about 1/20 scale) was going to be tough. Most are resin or white metal 54mm or 75mm figures of famous generals, emperors, etc. So I came up with a new plan, a Formula 1 figure in 1/20 scale by Tamiya. My calculating showed the size was right.

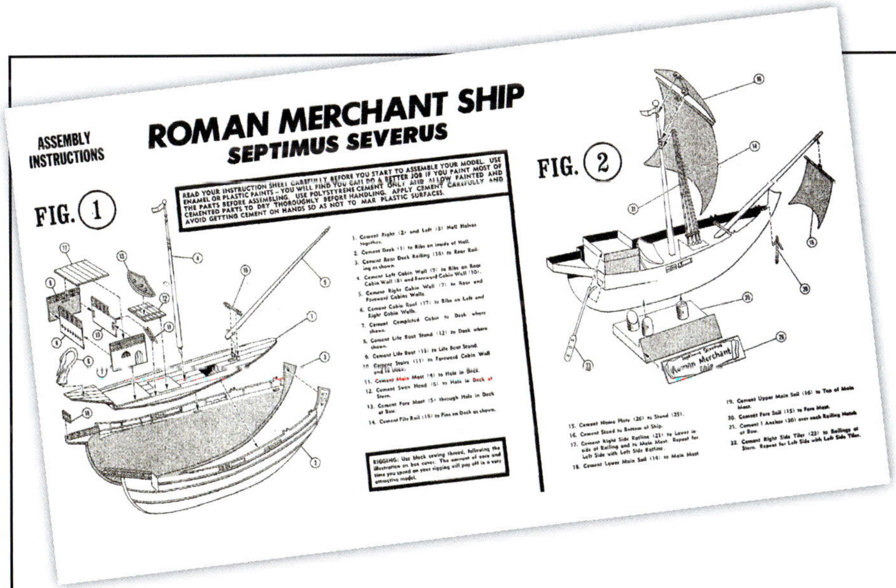

ASSEMBLY INSTRUCTIONS

ROMAN MERCHANT SHIP

SEPTIMUS SEVERUS

FIG. 1

FIG. 2

Roman Merchant

©PYRO PLASTICS CORP., 1967

15 Antique Ship INSTRUCTION SHEET

©PYRO PLASTICS CORP., 1968
PYRO PARK, UNION, NEW JERSEY
MADE AND PRINTED IN U.S.A.

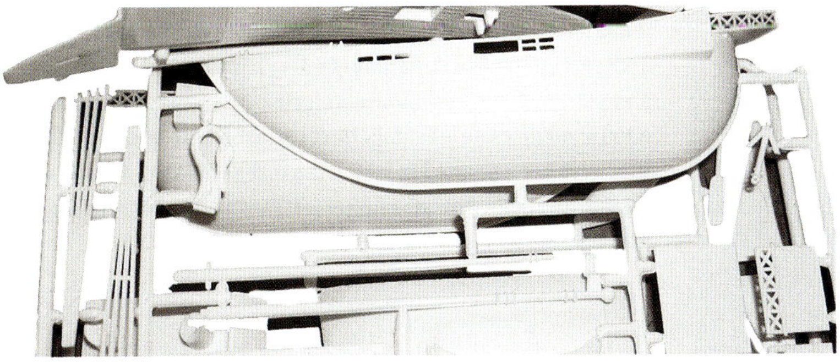

The kit's instructions are quite clear as the model can be assembled in just two steps as it contains less than 30 pieces. The ship's parts are cleanly molded with no deformities. The white plastic parts are well detailed.

## Phase I: The ship

I picked up the old (1968) Pyro kit at a store in Santa Cruz that I frequented for years, The kit can still be found at various websites. I like the kit because the plastic hull's wood texture is excellent as is the detailing of the deck, masts, and sails. Changes that were needed are small, primarily opening cargo hatches (see insert at right).

**Building the kit takes about 30 minutes. I then used Tamiya Putty dissolved in paint remover to fill holes and cover slots.**

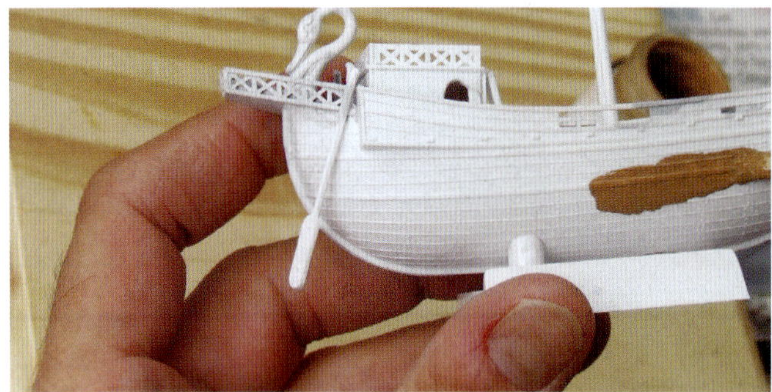

**Deck, masts, and sails are well detailed, so painting becomes key. I used diluted Tamiya Buff (XF-57) for the deck and hull. One layer is best for a detailed surface so as not to obscure the detail.**

**After the paint dried, I added a layer of Vallejo Brown Glaze (No. 70.854) to the hull, applying it with a No. 2 or No. 3 brush.**

**Finally, I dry-brushed the hull with Vallejo Dark Sand (No. 70.847) to add weathering and definition. Adding a wash with diluted black paint also can work and I've found careful use of a fine brush creates equally good shading as airbrushing. Next I attached the open cargo hatches that have been painted to match the rest of the ship, finally adding rigging and sails. The sails (lower left) are made of cloth dampened with a 50/50 solution of water and white glue.**

## Phase II: The ship terrace

I used hardwood for the terrace floor and balsa wood to create the railing for this element that would be used in the foreground, with the 1/20 scale figure. First, I marked the deck's slats with a ruler and scored the planks before adding indentations with a punch to represent pegs in the floor. Then, for the railing, I scored the balsa wood with a sharp No. 10 hobby blade before cutting out the rail pieces, using the classic "X" design used by Romans in their homes. **(1-3)**

To increase the richness of the wood's texture and to help it stand out in the diorama I applied a generous layer of reddish brown and black shoe polish. **(4)** I then let everything dry before finally sanding it with a coarse sandpaper to remove excess polish from the wood. **(5, 6)**

1

2

3

4

5

6

## Phase III: Roman senator

The Roman senator's form was already in my head when I started gathering pieces (arms, torsos, legs) from several figures, including Tamiya's Tire Changing Pit Crew (No. 20031). **(7)** Considering a toga would cover much of the body I could choose the appendages that best suited the pose.

After attaching those I started molding a tunic with two-part putty from Milliput. **(8)** I worked the folds with a slightly moistened No. 4 brush, then sanded with fine dampened

**Great patience is necessary for forming the senator's beard and hair with Tamiya two-part putty. Then it's painted with Vallejo Flat Brown (No. 70.984). Finally I decided to replace the original red trim of the toga with purple, using Blue Violet (No. 70.811).**

**12** Dock and port building · Docked boat · Small waves · Big wave · Stern of the ship leaving the port

sandpaper before completing it with a primer of diluted Tamiya Putty. **(9)**

Next I painted my newly created Roman figure's face, using Humbrol Matte Flesh (No. 061) while the eyes were painted with Vallejo Ivory (No. 70.918) and Olive Green (No. 70.967). I used Vallejo paints again for this diorama, unless otherwise noted.

Later I painted the toga Pure White (No. 69.001) and then added several washes of Black Glaze (No. 70.855) to create shadows on both the face and toga. **(10)** Once again I used Talens paint retardant to blend the whites and grays of the senator's clothing. **(11)**

## Phase IV: Forming the base and port

To reinforce the spacial progression here I divided the base into two distinct, equal-sized dioramas. **(12)** The first area would include the port building, the docked boat, the dock, and the sea around the ship. The second area was to be the stern of the ship leaving the harbor in the foreground, the Roman figure, and a big wave to help reinforce the depth of field and imply the ship's wake.

First, I cut a solid rectangle of white foam insulation nearly 2 inches thick and glued it to a wood base with white glue. To create the waves I applied Das Pronto (terracotta color) putty to start molding the waves, carefully keeping the waves a proper scale and not creating too much movement near the dock. The waves are roughly 0.2 inches tall. **(13-15)** In a few spots I added pieces of foam as a base to slightly increase wave volume.

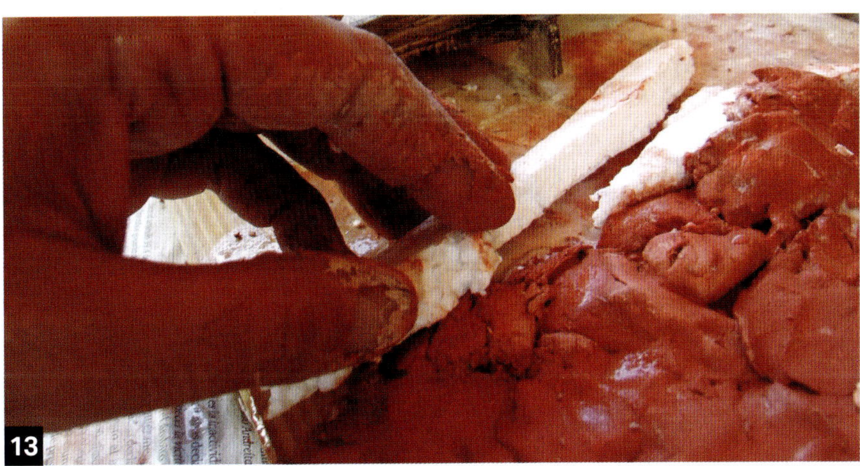

**13**

**14**

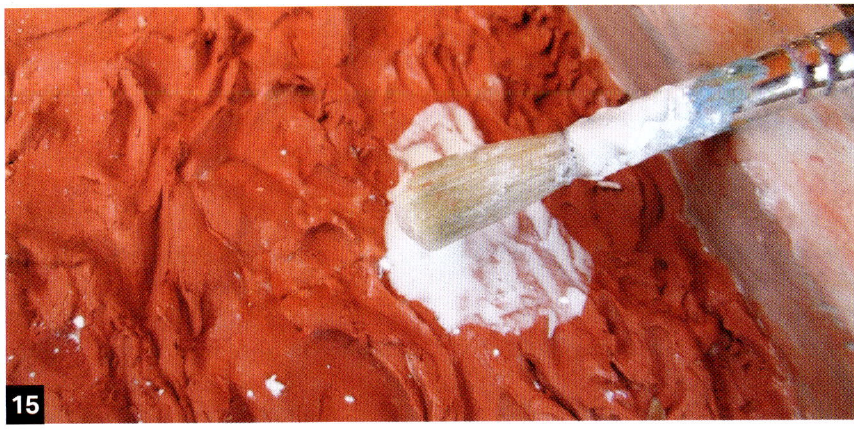

**15**

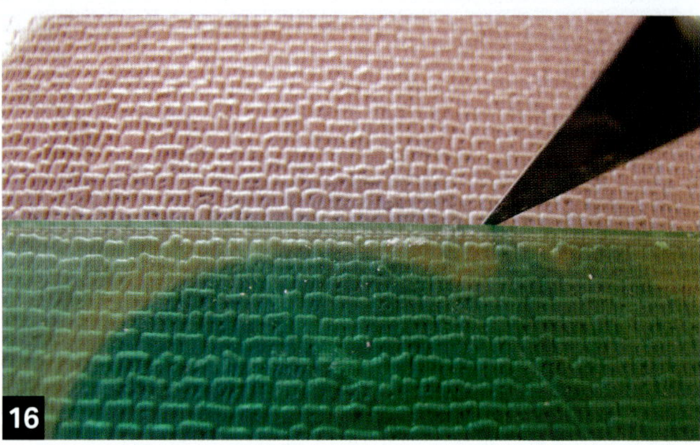
16

17

18

19

20

21

The front of the dock is a plastic sheet that imitates stone and is commonly used in model railroading layouts. I cut it to fit the dock's main wall which is about 11.8 inches long. **(16)** Then I built the port building **(17)** and raised the wall with the help of some pieces of chalk (yes, like we used at school years ago). **(18)** I formed the texture of the brick with a ruler and marked it with a pin. **(19)** Then I added wood and plastic details.

The port's road needs to imitate stone, which I accomplished by using molded stone pattern Evergreen sheet styrene, just 0.01-inch thick. I imitated the texture using a punch, while sticking the original base plate on white foam insulation. **(20)**

The port's roof was created with a pre-formed plastic sheet that mimics tile, again a model railroading accessory. **(21)** I decided to paint the port Light Gray (No. 70.990) except for the tile roof, which I painted with AK Interactive's Brick Red (No. 11093). **(22)** Next I coated everything with a layer of Black Glaze to weather the port.

I also used a sheet of Plasticard's Evergreen 0.04-inch styrene card to build a port warehouse. The roof features a base of German Red Brown (No. 71.271), tinged with a wash created from diluted brown mixed with black and finished with a dry-brushing of Orange (No. 71.083), just a tiny amount on the brush to add highlights.

22

**The port's columns are made with cotton swab sticks and attached with superglue.**

Capturing the vivid blue of the ocean is one of the prime challenges when creating a diorama that features the sea. But independent of the blues and greens one selects, the important thing is to correctly model the waves and apply a varnish that adds realistic highlights to the finished surface. After the paint dried I added Talens Acrylic Retarder.

23

FOAM TIP: Here's my trick to making realistic seafoam. Mix baking soda with white glue and apply it to the crests of the larger waves. This does not look right on smaller waves.

24

## Phase V: Painting the ocean

Finally, I painted the diorama's water surfaces with Ultramarine Blue (No. 72.022), then mixed the same blue with black and applied this mixture (diluted with water) in the waves' troughs. **(23)** I followed that with a mix of the Ultramarine Blue and a pinch of white to highlight the waves and then created foam with Pure White tinged with a wash of blue. **(24)**

Lastly I needed to create realistic waves to the sea port, so I used clear silicone adhesive and transparent glue (Imedio) to create foam and clear water. I used a dry brush with white to touch up the most roiled up white foam areas.

25

26

## Phase VI: Figures and port atmosphere

To add life to the port it needed a few figures, so I added five, all 1/160 scale Preiser figures. I chose the box of passengers and pedestrians (No. PR79006), and painted horses (No. PR79150) before placing a Roman soldier on a horse. Some of the poses were fine as they were, while a few required slight alterations. **(25, 26)**

The two women fit well in the dock's central area, which also includes a small terrace and a Roman banner.

## ABOUT THE AUTHOR

**Enrique Carrasco Molina** is a journalist, writer and professor of Advertising Communication at Universidad Europea de Canarias in the Canary Islands. He is a native of the Canary Islands and has published nine books related to communication and history, some focused on the study of sailing. He has been self-taught in modeling since he was 10, complementing the practice of the hobby with courses in Fine Arts (oil painting) and amateur work in 8mm cinema, and video, using self-made kits for science fiction short films. Between 1992 and 2000, he organized several competitions and exhibitions in collaboration with various specialized stores and town councils, contributing to the reactivation of the Tenerife Modelers Club. He has published numerous articles on modeling techniques in Spanish newspapers and also step-by-step articles in the Spanish magazine *Barcos, Modelismo y Radiocontrol* (Professional Magazines, 2007-2010). His dioramas also have appeared on the cover of *Barcos*. He has won several awards in modeling competitions, and since 2014 has been a senior consultant in various naval modeling workshops (Unodoce). At the beginning of 2021, he published the book *Sailing Ships and Dioramas* on Amazon Kindle Direct, in which he developed several step-by-step examples of naval dioramas for sailing ships. He also has written an academic article on the role of advertising for Revell since 1957. (Advertising communication of scale models as educational technical toys: case study of Revell's marketing strategy (1957-2022), printed in *Journal of Historical Research in Marketing*.)

## REFERENCES


*Small World: Dioramas in Contemporary Art*, Ashkin, M. & Kampe, T. (2000), Museum of Contemporary Art, San Diego

*Photographing Small-Scale Objects: History, Context and Format,* Brush, G. D. (1987), Leonardo, 20(3), 231-234.

*Natural History Dioramas, Shifting Paradigms of Natural History Diorama Background Painting*, pp 67-78, Anderson, Michael & James Perry Wilson (2015), Springer, Dordrecht.

*Technologies of Illusion: De Loutherbourg's Eidophusikon in Eighteenth-Century London*, Bermingham, A. (2016), Art History, 39(2), pp. 376-399.

*An Historical and Descriptive Account of the Various Processes of the Daguerréotype and the Diorama*, Daguerre, L. J. M. (1839), American Photographic Historical Society.

*L.J.M. Daguerre: The History of the Diorama and the Daguerreotype*, Gernsheim, H., & Gernsheim, A. (1968), p. 55, New York: Dover publication

*Dioramas as Constructs of Reality: Art, Photography, and the Discursive Space in Natural History Dioramas*, Howie, G. (2015), (pp. 39-65), Springer, Dordrecht.

*Natural History Dioramas*, Kamcke, C., & Hutterer, R. (2015), History of Dioramas (pp. 7-21), Springer, Dordrecht.

*Mirando dentro de la caja El Visor de dioramas con enfoque selectivo como caso práctico de arqueología de los medios,* Martínez, J. V. M. & Gauchía, I. A. (2018), "Media Archaeology," (Arqueología de los medios.)

*Analysis of a Natural History Exhibit: Are dioramas the answer?* International Journal of Museum Management and Curatorship, Peart, B., & Kool, R. (1988), 7(2), pp 117-128.

*What do dioramas tell visitors? A study at the History of Wildlife Diorama at the Museum of Scotland*, Tunnicliffe, S. D. (2008).

*Habitat Dioramas: Illusions of wilderness in museums of natural history*, Wonders, K. (1993), Uppsala: Uppsala University.

*The Diorama in Great Britain in the 1820s in History of Photography*, Wood, R. D. (1993), 17(3), pp 284-295.

*Walt Whitman and the Panorama, Walt Whitman Quarterly Review*, Zarobila, C. (1979), 25(2), 51.